P9-CQR-167

The
SHARK
and the
FISH

APPLYING POKER STRATEGIES
TO BUSINESS LEADERSHIP

CHARLEY SWAYNE

ECW Press

MIX
Paper from
responsible sources
FSC® C004071

Copyright © Charley Swayne, 2012

Published by ECW Press
2120 Queen Street East, Suite 200, Toronto, Ontario, Canada M4E 1E2
416-694-3348 / info@ecwpress.com

All rights reserved. No part of this publication may be reproduced,
stored in a retrieval system, or transmitted in any form by any process — electronic,
mechanical, photocopying, recording, or otherwise — without the prior written
permission of the copyright owners and ECW Press. The scanning, uploading, and
distribution of this book via the Internet or via any other means without the permission
of the publisher is illegal and punishable by law. Please purchase only authorized
electronic editions, and do not participate in or encourage electronic piracy of
copyrighted materials. Your support of the author's rights is appreciated.

LIBRARY AND ARCHIVES CANADA CATALOGUING IN PUBLICATION

Swayne, Charles B.
The shark and the fish : applying poker strategies to
business leadership / Charley Swayne.

ISBN 978-1-77041-027-5
Also issued as 978-1-77090-262-6 (PDF) and 978-1-77090-263-3 (ePub)

1. Leadership. 2. Decision making. 3. Poker--Economic aspects. I. Title.

HD57.7.S94 2012   658.4'092   C2012-902769-3

Cover and text design: Tania Craan
Cover image: © pavlen / iStockphoto
Typesetting: Kendra Martin
Printing: Webcom 1 2 3 4 5

Printed and bound in Canada

No man has ever had a more wonderful wife than Carol or better sons than Joe, Brian, and Chuck.

CONTENTS

1

Introduction

My mission is *to help you make better decisions than you would have made on your own.* Every day for over a year I wrote that mission at the top of the page. Then I got to work. Great news: if there isn't a precise roadmap, there is a lighthouse guiding you to a higher level of strategic thinking and decision making.

Answers have been found. Theory has been translated so you can use it. According to the *Wall Street Journal,* the most sought-after leadership skill is strategic thinking. This book will help you to go about making the wisest possible decision and pulling the trigger.

Building a company is really hard. Leading the company is all about creating an environment in which anyone in the organization would make the same decision and take the same action you would if you were there. And it's about giving them the freedom to do so.

Why poker and business? I often use poker as a metaphor because I have found that world-class poker players think in an entirely different way than good players — they really do think strategically. Great leaders also think in a different way than good managers. It was no coincidence that Gates launched Microsoft, Nixon funded his first campaign, and Eisenhower paid for his military uniforms — all from their poker winnings. The skill is not the cards or business; it's a higher dimension of creating an extraordinary environment, and you are about to find out what it is and how to do it.

We will start by discovering your compass. We will look into the future, create a mission, set objectives, determine strategies, take action, and then evaluate, experiment, and adapt.

As a bonus, if you lead a business or organization, you'll see how to instill in your people the sense that "we did it" (the workers) as opposed to "they did it" (the managers). And, when that happens, you will discover ever-increasing possibilities.

Let's roll.

The Leader Makes It Happen

Leader as savior. Leader as messiah. Leader as hero. Atlantis fulfilled. It's all a crock. The leader is not the wizard behind the curtain pulling all the right levers. The leader is not some seductive siren song. This image is nothing more than a self-serving myth.

If you think you're in charge, you're not even close. Your authority is limited. There is no cosmic chess board. As Philip Gelatt, president of Northern Engraving, said after 40 years in business, "It doesn't matter what I do. I can't control anything."

At dinner one day, one of our children asked me what we were going to do on the weekend. I carefully explained to them, "There is one vote per person in this family. I have one, and your mom has the rest."

Despite what your span of control looks like on your organizational chart, control does not really exist. The longer the span, the shorter

> *Shift the power to the folks bringing in the beans. — Colin Powell*

the control. The greater the tooth-to-tail ratio, the lesser the command. It's not the person at the top, it's the people within. The organization is bottom up, inside out. Organizations manage themselves. None of us has ever done it on our own. That doesn't mean we don't need top management; it's just that top management needs to embrace that it's not only top down but also bottom up. The day is saved or lost by those on the ground.

Okay, now that you have the bad news, there *is* good news. Leadership is less about command and control and more about creation. You are the base that influences the pH of your company's soil. You have the power to create character-based leadership.

True leadership is when you create an atmosphere in which your people are so engaged that, when faced with unforeseen circumstances and forces, they act as you would and in some cases better than you would. Freeing the energies of the hive. A multiplier effect. More later.

Police officer Rick Hanna was working out on a stair climber at the Gainesville Health and Fitness Center. He fell off. Patrick, the supervisor, went over, and Rick said, "I just need to rest for a moment." But then he passed out. No heartbeat. A sudden-death cardiac event. Immediately, Patrick started CPR; Kristen, the saleswoman, gave him mouth to mouth; and David from maintenance went for the AED (automatic external defibrillator) and literally broke his hand ripping it off the wall. Still no pulse, but they kept working on Rick. Within 10 minutes, the paramedics arrived. The officer was dead. The paramedics continued to work on him for another 20 minutes, and finally they got a heartbeat. At the hospital, when he woke up, Rick was fine. Amazingly, no brain damage. In the words of Marlene Hanna, his wife, "The cardiologists and pulmonary doctors all say the same thing, had it not happened in your gym, he would not be alive today, and because your staff were so well trained and you had the AED equipment right there. Most importantly, no one gave up. They continued CPR well after the paramedics arrived."

Joe Cirulli owns the Gainesville Health and Fitness Center. You might have seen him on the cover of *Inc.* magazine. Joe wasn't present, but his leadership was. I have seen Joe when faced with an emergency, and that's exactly what he would have done if he was there. His staff reacted exactly the way he would have.

Business School

More good news and bad news. First the bad news.

How many times have you heard of a board hiring a professor to run their company? If you took away the textbook from a business professor, what would he do in the classroom? Nothing. He would have no idea what to do. He can't leap beyond what he knows. He has never been a business manager. He has never had to make a profit. He has no experience, no anchor. Academics can't go beyond what they know. For the most part, they don't know anything except what is in the textbook. It is the difference between being in the stands and playing on the field.

When doing research for this book, I refused to interview any academic whose only life had been at a university. Although many are nice, intelligent people, they live in a world of their own, a silo, without authentic experience. They have no clue about what they have no clue. They will always hire the green PhD as opposed to the experienced businessman, worrying more about accreditation than quality. They write incestuous, dust-gathering, refereed research papers for other theorists to say "attaboy"; and, once they are tenured, they forget about hard work. On a Friday afternoon, if we still had phone booths, you could put all the professors who are actually on campus into one.

What would happen if the White House hired no one but academics to run the country? I guess we know the answer to that one.

We give students a brick of information, followed by another brick, followed by another brick, followed by another brick, until they graduate, at which point we assume they have a house. What they have is a pile of bricks, and they don't have it for long (Krohn).

Business school is nothing but a ticket to the dance. The rules you learn are a betrayed promise. Warren Buffett has it right: "Beware of geeks bearing formulas." No company ever faces a generic problem; it faces a specific problem. It's not that the bricks

> *The only thing that interferes with my learning is my education.*
> — *Albert Einstein*

of the business rules, the maxims, the models don't matter; they do. They just don't matter as much as we think they do. They all sound good, but they don't have much value in the real world. Powell: "Management techniques are not magic mantras but simply tools to be reached for at the right times." Business school starts with cherished management theories and shoves the facts into those theories. Practice always deviates from theory.

Although I have tried to distinguish between relevant and irrelevant concepts, and give only the most important bricks, there is no prescriptive formula. We do not live in a world with simple linear cause and effect. We cannot control or fully understand the vagaries of the marketplace. Equilibrium taught in the texts seldom occurs; disequilibrium is the norm. There is nothing that reduces our businesses or personal lives to science.

Now the good news. If you understand the house, you can understand the bricks. If all you can do is understand the bricks, then you'll never understand the house. We will look at the house, not just at the bricks, and add some mortar. By the time we are finished, you will have a better understanding of which is which.

> *When a subject becomes totally obsolete, we make it a required course.*
> — *Peter Drucker*

Model versus Reality

I use models a lot (not the runway kind — I've been married for almost 50 years), both visual and verbal. Models are perfect; reality isn't.

You'll see some new ones here. The three most important are the Strategic-Thinking, Knowledge, and Decision-Making models. For the most part, the elements of these models aren't original, but you might find the systematic progression of the elements new.

Most of the models are two dimensional; a few are three dimensional. Matrices oversimplify. They are useful for understanding a point but do not come anywhere close to capturing reality. Reality is multi-dimensional, with imprecise definitions, unknown knowledge, and unseen interactions.

Some exceptional strategic thinkers have done all of this naturally, without effort, their entire lives. They are the exceptions. Their brains are prewired with patterns of thought linking strategy, tactics, and moral reasoning (Gilkey, Caceda, and Kilts). The Strategic-Thinking, Knowledge, and Decision-Making models are for the rest of us; they are helpful checklists to make sure we have covered everything. The more you use them, the more routine and natural they become. Eventually, you won't even have to think about them.

You might have seen the model of Know and Don't Know (Figure 1.1).

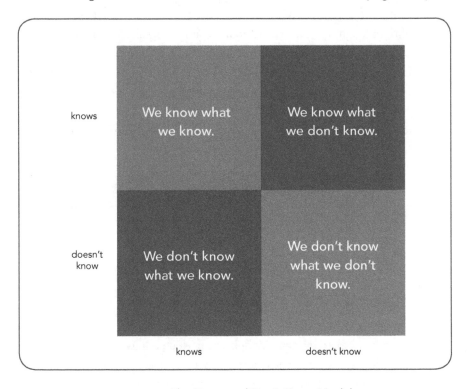

	knows	doesn't know
knows	We know what we know.	We know what we don't know.
doesn't know	We don't know what we know.	We don't know what we don't know.

Figure 1.1 The Know and Don't Know Model

One thing only I know, and that is I know nothing. — *Socrates*

This model says there are those who know what they know, know what they don't know, don't know what they know, and don't know what they don't know, such as the professor without real-world experience.

Here's the reality (Figure 1.2).

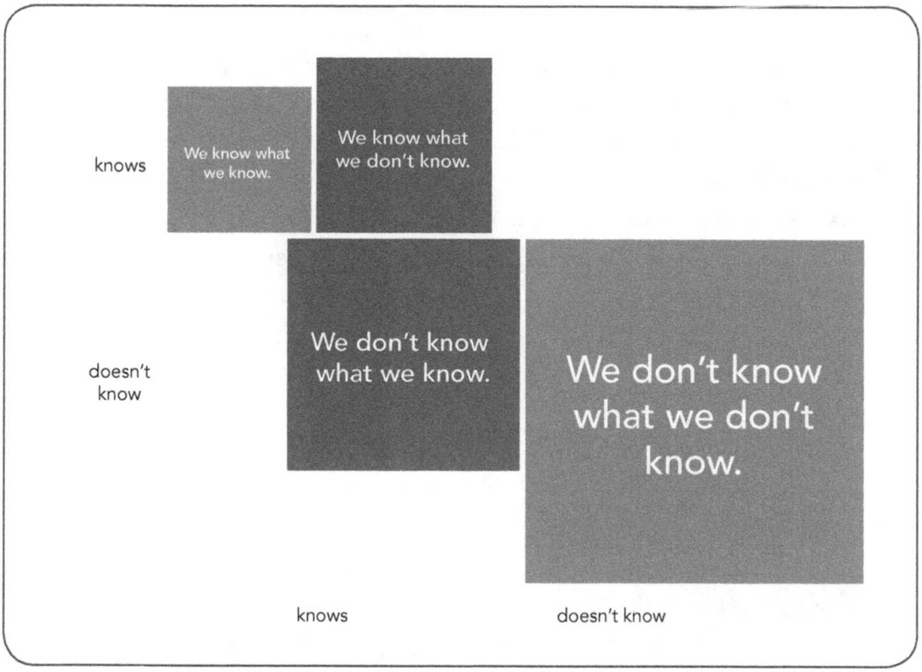

Figure 1.2 The Know and Don't Know Reality

What we don't know about what we don't know is huge. Far greater than we think. As we gather information and knowledge and make decisions, always remember how many times we don't even know what we don't know.

We don't know one-millionth of one percent about anything.
— *Thomas Edison*

Critical Thinking

"Critical thinking" is a term bandied about in universities. What's the difference between strategic thinking and critical thinking? Who cares? There are some scholarly differences, but when you boil it down to its essence, critical thinking is solving a problem and making a decision.

Why Poker?

Poker is a game of trying to make the wisest decisions, with imperfect information, usually with only a small edge over your opponents, and forcing your competitors to make difficult decisions. Poker expands the strategic thinking of those who are specialized in what they do and reinforces how to make difficult decisions for those who have to do so all the time.

Both business and poker appear to be simple games. Just make sure your revenues exceed your expenses. Just make sure you have the best hand. But with more subtleties than the novice imagines, both are far more complex. There's an old axiom that poker isn't a card game played by people; it's a people game played with cards. Well, business isn't a money game played by people; it's a people game played with time, talent, and treasure.

Mike Sexton, host of the World Poker Tour, World Series of Poker bracelet winner with over $3.8 million in tournament winnings: "If you approach poker by thinking of it as running a business, you are going to do much better in poker than the average guy will do. In the business world you are constantly gathering information and making decisions. You invest your money and hope to get a return on your investment. Playing poker is the exact same thing."

Howard Lederer, two-time World Series of Poker bracelet winner with over $1.5 million in tournament winnings: "Poker is a series of difficult decisions under conditions of uncertainty."

Charlie Nesson, Harvard law professor and founder of the Global Poker Strategic Thinking Society: "Poker is the quintessential strategic game. The point at which you start to play poker is the point at which you are more interested in what is around you. The point where you look to see what is happening in the environment is where the game starts."

Avery Cardoza, CEO of Cardoza Publishing, the world's leader in poker books: "Poker is the only game that combines luck and psychology." That's a business environment.

Lyle Berman, CEO of many businesses, founder of the World Poker Tour, and three-time bracelet winner: "Poker has made me a more competent businessperson. It helps keep my mind sharp and reminds me that every decision I make has ramifications."

Tony Hsieh, CEO of Zappos.com: "I noticed so many similarities between poker and business that I started making a list of the lessons I learned from playing poker that could also be applied to business."

Why Texas Hold'em?

Poker is to checkers as Texas Hold'em is to chess. Of all the variations of poker, Texas Hold'em requires a high degree of skill and most closely resembles business since decisions must be made under extreme uncertainty by combining probabilities (pot odds, implied odds, expected value), psychology (aggressiveness, hand reading, tells), limited resources (chip stack, bankroll management), public information (the board, the bets, the calls, the raises), proprietary information (hole cards, both opponents' and yours), and luck. As you learn Texas Hold'em, you learn a language and a thought process that can be applied to much more complicated business situations.

The most valuable and business-applicable aspect of poker is how it teaches us to look at things from another's point of view. The ability to put ourselves in the moccasins of our customers, employees, and competitors and understand not just *what* they think but also *why* they think the way they do is something we can use for the rest of our lives.

Texas Hold'em is part of the culture of global investment trading firm Susquehanna International Group; it wants "to teach people how to be good decision makers under uncertainty" (McCauley). Kia Mohajeri, a consistent placer in many tournaments, with over $1 million in poker winnings, argues that "Hold'em is a combination of science, art, [and] psychology." The same can be said for business.

If you don't already know how to play Texas Hold'em, go to Appendix B.

Metaphors

"I'm a pretty good poker player," Barack Obama has freely admitted. He is elected overwhelmingly. He immediately multi-tables (war, cap and trade, Gitmo, health care, family). He is looking at the health-care table with pocket Aces (his mandate) and flops an Ace (a majority in the House and Senate). He makes a good bet (but not enough to get the Republicans to fold), assumes he has this hand won, and focuses on the other tables. On the turn, the Republicans catch their inside straight (the Brown Massachusetts victory). Obama reads the board correctly and sees that his opponents have caught, but he is pot committed (with so much political capital) and shoves. On the river, the board pairs, and he wins.

Twain-Swayne. I never met a four I didn't like. My puns, which at maturity are fully groan, humor (or lack of it), and metaphors appear now and then. Like my wife and sons, you just need to read over them.

> *Samuel Clemens chose Mark Twain as his pen name from his time as an apprentice on Mississippi steamboats. He would be at the bow with a weighted line and call off the depth of the river to the captain. A mark is a fathom, six feet. Twain means two. If the depth of the river was 12 feet, he'd call out, "Mark Twain."*

Poker versus Business

There are some major differences between poker and business. The first is that, while lying is necessary at the poker table, in business it's a recipe for disaster. When we die, we should be proud of the way we played our lives. The second is that, while poker is about 70% skill and 30% luck, business is far more complicated and, other than hard work and persistence, at most is 50% skill and 50% luck. In too many cases, it is 1% skill and 99% luck. The third is that, unlike business, poker is essentially a one-person business. No customers. No employees. As soon as customers, employees, and stakeholders are added into the equation, everything becomes complex.

A few talented poker players can use their thought processes to become business executives. The key word is *few*. Although the greats do possess strategic-thinking and decision-making skills, some are degenerate gamblers and action junkies who can't make the transition to executive leadership. But aggressive, strategic-thinking business leaders who are experienced decision makers can make the transition to great poker play. Recent World Series of Poker bracelet winners include a TV producer, a patent attorney, an accountant, an investment banker, and a carpet manufacturer (MacMillan).

> *Poker results usually occur within 30 seconds, but in business it may take years.* — Lyle Berman

> *If someone's been successful at poker, then there's a good chance they could be successful in business.* — Danon Robinson

The universes are not parallel, but the connections are real if sometimes subtle. For example, theoretically, every poker player will eventually receive every possible hand, against every type of opponent, in every position, with similar chip stacks, in every possible situation. Obviously, this isn't true in business.

Poker is a zero-sum game. Often in business we don't have to adopt the enemy syndrome where we try to eliminate every opponent; rather, we gain when we have a relatively high market share with many competitors.

I'll point out other areas where there are differences, but the similarities, especially in negotiation and deal making, far outweigh the dissimilarities.

Market Development

If you stayed awake in business school, you'll recall the term "market development" means taking an existing product and selling it to a new market. Orange juice isn't just for breakfast anymore. The term can also denote expanding your brand to new customers (Figure 1.3).

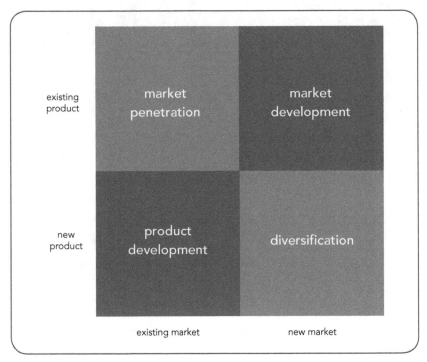

Figure 1.3 Market Product Matrix

Bayer Aspirin went beyond headaches and expanded its market as a blood thinner, reducing the chances of a heart attack. UST Global, a provider of IT services, expanded into India. Unilever extended its Dove brand to the men's market with its Men+Care soap, deodorant, and body wash products. Apple has many products, such as the iPhone, that were originally targeted for the consumer market; now it is finding ways to use the same product but in the business-to-business market.

Here market development will mean more. It's not just what you spend in the traditional marketing model below (Figure 1.4). It's the sum of all resources spent by you and your competitors to create a product, to make potential customers aware of it, to put it in the right location, and to hire the right people, and it's all of the other aspects necessary to develop a market. When many different organizations are simultaneously appealing to a market, demands and needs, not just products, are formed.

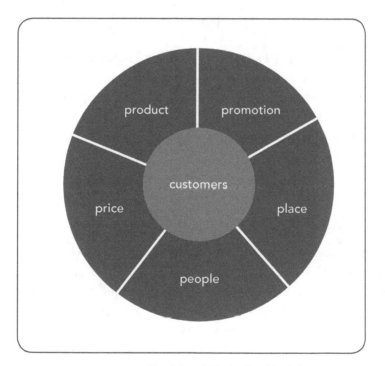

Figure 1.4 Traditional Marketing Model

We would all love to be DeBeers, to influence supply and therefore price. There are times when you want competitors to develop the market, when the process of adoption is speeded up, so you don't have to do all of the work and commit all of the resources yourself.

Market development will also mean advancing a brand. All of us think of individual business brands such as Jell-O, L'eggs, Coke, Budweiser, McDonald's, or umbrella business brands such as General Motors, Nike, General Electric, and Johnson & Johnson. Today we must also include personal brands such as Negreanu, Jordan, and Oprah. Daniel Negreanu has created an aura of the smart, likable winner and been able to foster that brand in a number of related business ventures. Michael Jordan is known for being a champion, cool under pressure, and having an off-court sense of humor. Lady O's brand is one of a kind.

Greatness

Great players are great because they play solid fundamental poker and learn from their mistakes. They do not win because they get great cards; they win because they play their cards great. Great leaders are great because they are experienced in the fundamentals, and they too learn from their mistakes. They sense when to aggressively seize an opportunity and when to back down.

Some Analogies

A hand in a cash game can be thought of as a one-time stock trade, negotiation, or business transaction. You are trying either to win the most or to lose the least while learning something about your opponents you can use later. Playing a cash game for several hours is similar to engaging in a series of stock trades. You are trying to win the most or lose the least over a short period of time.

We all remember the product life cycle as seen on the next page (Figure 1.5). A hand in a no-limit tournament can be thought of as the life cycle of an individual product.

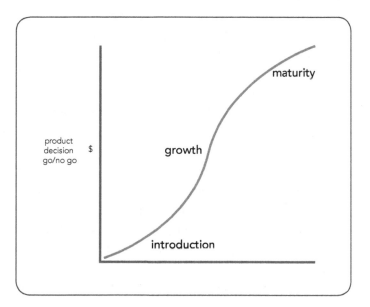

Figure 1.5 Product Life Cycle

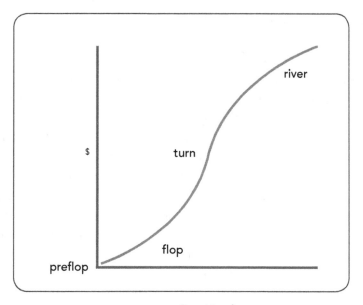

Figure 1.6 One Hand

You invest and take some risks throughout the various stages of the life cycle (the betting rounds). You constantly obtain more information (how strong you are compared with your competitors), manage finances (your chip stack and personal bankroll), and make decisions about whether to keep investing or exit the market (Figure 1.6).

A no-limit tournament, from start to end, is the life cycle of a business division. It's the sum of the hands you play in the tournament. If we added together the graphs of all of our individual products, then we'd have our company's life cycle.

The pot can be thought of as both market share and what's at stake with a product. Profit is part of what's at stake, and the higher your market share generally the greater the profit. The pot also holds your organization's time, talent, and treasure. Finally, every pot also contains something more, the essence of why you are in business, which we will discuss in more depth later.

Pots go up geometrically on the turn — that is, the market growth phase. Costs rise. Critical decisions are made whether to stay in and call (new plant and equipment, more research and development), raise and try to push competitors out (all-in advertising to increase market share and in turn profits), or fold. With greater risk, the potential reward becomes greater.

Customers determine the winner of the pot in business, the cards in poker. Unlike poker, where a split pot is rare, you can often have a graduated split pot with your product, depending on your relative market share. In business, you don't have to run every competitor out of business to have a nice slice of the pie. In poker, you want the whole pie.

Many more analogies are easy to make. Preflop is getting the restaurant ready for the morning opening, preliminary research, or customer feedback on product testing before launch. The flop could be taking the restaurant order, a personal trainer writing up the workout for a new client, or bidding on a major project. The turn would be the busy dinner crowd, the deal that is close to consummation, or taking your company public. The river could include cleaning the restaurant after closing, accepting or declining a position of employment, or year-end results. The pot would be time spent on sales calls, objects traded, and of course money invested.

A Lifetime of Poker Playing

Poker players lead unusual lives. More ups and downs than an oscilloscope. Rich one day, broke the next. I've said a tournament is analogous to a division's life cycle. Your company's life cycle is the sum of the life cycles of all of your divisions.

Each product or division is not an end in itself but a piece in building a great company. And there is so much more to life than your company. If there were graphs for your family, friends, and spiritual life, they would be superimposed onto the one for your company's life.

About the Book

To help you make prudent decisions, we will first understand strategic thinking (Figure 1.7). Next we will examine the knowledge necessary to think strategically. Then we will apply both strategic thinking and knowledge to a practical but extensive decision-making process that can be used by any leader. Finally, we will discuss how to create an organizational environment that magnifies what you could ever do on your own.

I will briefly go over some basics. I fully understand, if you are in a leadership position today, you know all of this. The reviewed basics and the obvious statements are for those who might not have the background you do, but some might give new meanings to things you already know.

We want to see the whole at a glance, be 30,000 feet above the ground, but you can't see all the details from that high. You have to land to see what's really going on. I might get too technique specific now and then, and every once in a while I will digress from the topic at hand. I'll do so only when I have a relevant point to make or a story to share.

At times, you'll see I'm being too pokerish, providing more detail than might seem necessary. I won't always connect the dots. And some statements might not seem relevant the first time you go through the book, but when you come back for a reread you'll realize why I included them.

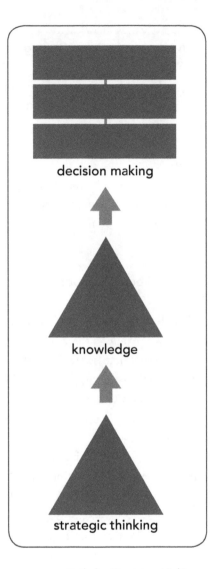

decision making

knowledge

strategic thinking

Figure 1.7 Path for Decision Making

I will flip between talking about you and your business or organization. You will have to interchange them mentally to apply to what you are reading. Almost all of the puzzle pieces mean the same thing whether applied to you or a company, but a few here and there will apply only to you or a business/organization.

My idea density will not be consistent: sometimes I will use a few pages to make a minor point; other times I will make a reflective truth in a one-liner. In class, I overstate or embellish some things to make sure students get the point. Same here. Some examples and quotations are from my memory. When you get to be my age, you'll find that's not always accurate. If it didn't happen, it should have.

You'll find many snapshots as opposed to videos. I'll introduce ideas that could easily be expanded into a full chapter or even a separate book. My purpose in doing so is not to dwell on the intricacies of a topic but to give you a point of departure if it piques your interest. If I expanded every thought to its conclusion, you'd get a hernia lifting this book.

Strange how people use the same words to mean different things. I will use comfortable and familiar words either because esoteric language would cause you to throw down the book or I couldn't come up with a better word to dig into a deeper meaning. It's important you understand what I mean when I use a word or term, so I will usually define what I mean or give specific examples.

Poker players usually don't know squat about business leaders and vice versa. Unless the people are known worldwide, the first time they are mentioned I will include a few words about who they are. When I mention a title, such as CEO, it could mean either a current or a former position. After someone is introduced, I'll often just refer to him by last name. Appendix D has everyone quoted and a little about him.

In later chapters, if you think you are reading something you read before, you are right. I will sometimes repeat myself either because I think it is important or because it is necessary to make a point. One thing I will repeat often. Unlike a book on thermodynamics, where the last chapter is a progressive culmination of each of the previous chapters, things in business and life are not nearly as smooth. And I can't present them as smooth. Most of the concepts aren't linear, one building on another. They are messy, intertwined, mixed. I'll present models in a linear fashion, but nothing in life is that simple. Circumstances and thought processes continually change, requiring looping around and around, jumping from one part to another and from one model to another.

There are some answers. Like the law of gravity, most answers are, and always have been, in plain view. Except not everyone can see them. Every time we discover something and get an answer, it often brings up more questions. I might not know the answers, but I usually know the questions. Probative questions are sometimes more important than immediate answers, and they help one to think in the abstract, to bring what's in the back of the mind to the front, to uncover, clarify, and lead to more judicious than impulsive decisions.

You'll find I use "he" and "him," but they're also generic for "she" and "her." In this politically correct world, no offense is meant, and I hope none is taken. I will also use "staff" and "employees" for your people, even though I know many organizations use "associates," "cast members," "team members," "soldiers," "customer wizards," "cross-utilization agents," "sandwich makers," or any of several other descriptions to reflect their particular corporate culture. I write as I talk, not in formal, complete sentences, sometimes using improper grammar, and even making up new words.

I can't fulfill my mission to help you make better decisions than you would have made on your own if I play the PC game. This book won't be politically correct thanks to Jack David, owner of ECW Press. He allowed me to say what I wanted to say. You might think that is usual.

When Simon and Schuster said they wanted to publish my book *What a College Senior Should Know When the Party Is Over and the Barrel Is Empty*, I was overjoyed. That joy didn't last. They threw out the chapter on "Lawyers, Politicians, and the Press," changed the title to *Life, Etc.* They turned an edgy discussion into pabulum. So I won't say "too big to fail" when I really mean "paying off politicians." I'm going to say what I think you need to hear, not what you want to hear. I will state the truth as I see it. I'm sure my comments about business professors and degen poker players won't go over well with some I know.

You can accept or reject anything. Everything is like an ornament for a Christmas tree (the university would call it a holiday tree, and of course they wouldn't have an angel on the top). You can put on the ones you like and leave off the ones you don't.

When I read something, I am distracted by footnotes, so I don't use them; rather, you'll see endnotes at the back of the book. When you see quotation marks, don't always take them as precise; they are sometimes my selective shading of what the person meant. Every once in a while, you'll see a sidebar containing some related trivia or quotation.

I don't claim to be a great poker player, strategic thinker, or businessman. But I'm better than the average bear. I am a good decision maker because I am experienced. Experience is what counts. The sidebar below explains how I got my experience. What I am really good at is questioning the best and getting their answers. And then teaching to others what they have taught me.

> *Trivia is from Latin, meaning "three roads."*
> *Each week some men would meet where the*
> *three roads met and tell stories to each other.*

> *Good decisions come from experience,*
> *and experience comes from bad decisions.*

What you are about to read are the thoughts of those wiser than me. I have tried to fill in the tremendous gap between the idealized view and a practical way of getting there so the information is useful to you.

2

Strategic Thinking

In the next chapter, we will start to understand how poker thinking can enhance your business skills. This chapter on strategic thinking is a foundation for anyone trying to understand anything. The next few pages won't involve much poker.

I view strategic thinking as your best attempt, and I emphasize *attempt*, to put a puzzle together when you can't see the picture on the box, where there are no edges to the puzzle, where there are extra pieces, and where some pieces are missing. Many pieces are three dimensional, and the shapes are constantly changing. To top it off, you are working on several different puzzles at the same time. In business and poker, Rich Horwath notes, we can think of it as the continual habit of gaining insights to understand the puzzle pieces to reach a competitive advantage. Figure 2.1 is the general Strategic-Thinking model with the main puzzle pieces. We will go through each part of the pyramid.

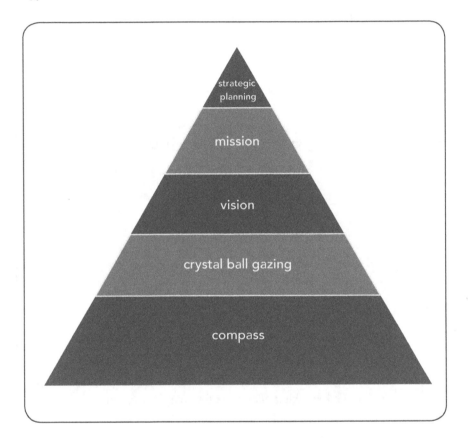

Figure 2.1 Strategic-Thinking Model

Your Personal Compass

Your personal compass is composed of two parts: principles and gifts. Let's examine each.

Your Reason for Being

The two most important days in your life are the day you were born and the day you discover why you were born.

Some people don't think past lunch, much less try to learn about their inner selves. Discovering your prime directive isn't easy. In fact, most of us never fully discover our raison d'être, why we were born. We can't easily change our reasons for being, so we might as well try to find out what they are.

As you might expect, whatever you find will probably stay constant throughout your lifetime. If you find good, then most likely you'll remain good; if you find evil or destruction, then it will take a traumatic event, an epiphany, or a deep desire to change. For most people, parents (mostly nature, some nurture) and cultural traditions turn out to be the primary shapers of who we are.

Here are some of the driving forces in people's lives. Several overlap with one another.

Greed	Respect	Independence
Self-gratification	Reputation	Accomplishment
Addiction	Prestige	Education and
Pleasure	Fame	learning
Cruelty	Beauty	Family
Hate	Experiences, fun,	Competition
Revenge	excitement	Self-actualization
Worry	Leisure time	and fulfillment
Doubt	Social	Honor
Fear	Kindness	Courage
Obligation	Love	Growing
Guilt	Health	organizations
Jealousy	Deal making,	Creating
Pride	bargaining,	Discovering
Power	negotiating	Imagining
Wealth	Leadership	Mentoring
Possessions	Professional or	Service to others
Living arrangements	career	Spiritual or religious

How do you discover what your deepest instincts and feelings are? In the words of that great philosopher Elmer Fudd, "Vewwy, vewwy swowly." The awakening can't be rushed. Speedaholics and those stuck in fast forward need not apply.

Few have ever had an epiphany, one life-changing event, that pulled back the curtain to reveal their inner cores. The inner self is usually discovered layer by layer. Often there is an obstacle between each tier. You "swowly" come closer to the white light of personal enlightenment but can't see everything it shines on, seldom fully understanding your center.

The most effective method of discovering each layer is meditation. It has been used for thousands of years but has been lost in today's busy society. Used daily, it reduces stress, allows both the mind and the body to relax, gives inner peace, but most importantly reveals your core.

We actually have two brains. Our left brain can be thought of as our ego. It is the one that focuses on "me." The right brain is silent. It controls our emotions. It provides connections with others. It is the brain that focuses on "we" and exposes who we really are.

As you use meditation to reach your relaxed spiritual state, focus on your heart, the mental extension of your right brain. Imagine looking into your heart to see what's there. This takes real effort since you probably have no idea what you're looking for when you begin or even that you've begun looking toward your inner self. It can come from artistic endeavors that bring about a meditative state, it can be purposeful (e.g., I'm going to meditate now), it can be a floating of the subconscious.

At first, it might be difficult to uncover anything, or whatever you do find might be unclear or vague. However, if you keep looking, steadily, consistently, you'll find something. It might be a small thing initially. It might take a long time before you uncover the meaning of what you have found, but little by little you will hear the voice that resounds in all of us. Eventually, you'll begin to gain an understanding of your core being. You'll be able to feel the roots of your inner self stretching wide and deep.

I'm sure you noticed some of the driving forces listed on the previous page are superficial. If that's true for you, I suggest you keep digging. Perhaps you will find a deeper layer; however, some of us never find that center.

Hopefully, you uncover a good soul, a voice that tells you why you are here, what's right from wrong. A voice that values peace, harmony, generosity, justice, integrity, truth — the true questions of life. The basis for character-based leadership. Your core does not change with the situation no matter what. It defines why you exist. It forms the rules that determine what you do. It isn't composed of just "shall nots"; it also has a lot of "shalls." Whatever you discover, don't shade it, and don't hide it. Simply live it. It won't go away. Living true to yourself gives you genuine happiness.

The more layers you uncover, the more your subconscious takes over. Things go on autopilot. You believe with the core of your being where you are going. You spend more time with like-minded people. Your intuition becomes correct. You see more opportunities. You develop more clarity, more confidence. You have more fun. You laugh more. Why? Your inner soul directs your brain, and your brain directs every action of every cell. Each cell of your body has a purpose and a memory. That purpose is your guiding force.

Many find that, if their driving force is building wealth, they lose spirit. It becomes a hollow game with soulless riches, leading to extreme excess. When your driving force is more than that, a way to leave your mark on the world, though it might result in wealth, you find it fulfilling and fun. Where your treasure is, that's where your heart is.

After a day of watching Mother Teresa care for the poor, the sick, and the extremely disfigured, a visitor said to her, "I wouldn't do that for a million dollars." She replied, "I wouldn't do that for a million dollars either."

What happens when you deal with others and are unsure of which side they fall on? Offer your hand in peace if he will unclench his fist. But once you find someone who has a Gekko or Scarface dark soul, one who is out to get you or your organization, you cannot hope he just implodes on his own. In a later chapter, we will discuss "fight on."

Changing Your Behavior

Before you think I'm being too romantic, too kumbaya-ish, I said *hopefully* you find good in there. Do you play by the rules, or do you think the rules are to be broken? There is a struggle between good and evil in all of us. Eventually, if you don't know it already, you will know on which side you fall. If it's on the dark side, it is possible to change, *but only if you want to*.

Behavior is a result of thoughts. The more important the thought, the more it dominates action. Repeated thoughts become embedded in the subconscious, resulting in habitual conduct. If we want to change our behavior, we must change what is fixed in our subconscious. How? We control our conscious thoughts. One specific repeated thought dominates all others. A repeated conscious thought eventually makes it way into the subconscious, and then that new thought becomes behavior. Paraphrasing Aristotle, "We become what we repeatedly think."

Can it possibly be that simple? Yes. If you have never used this technique, just try it consistently, relentlessly, for a few months (paraphrasing the thoughts of Napoleon Hill).

Let's suppose you are messy, unorganized. Every day handwrite "I am organized" on a sheet of paper. Read it aloud to yourself several times a day. Within a few months, you'll see a remarkable change. Once you are satisfied with your new, organized self, try changing another bad habit.

Or you are just learning poker. "I play only premium hands in early position."

If you don't make good decisions, handwrite and repeat daily "I make the wisest decision possible given its importance and the time available."

Note that the statements of desired action are in the present, not the future, tense. As an aside, this works best if you change one behavior at a time.

Changing Your Core

After you have changed relatively easy behaviors, and have seen how clear-cut the results are, you are ready to focus on the most important driving force you wish to change. Prepare to spend months before you see the change. For example, "Every action I take is based on integrity."

People can shape the person they want to become *if they **really** want to and change their conscious thoughts* by writing down, reading aloud, and repeating the desired conduct over and over until it becomes a subconscious habit.

Your Authentic Identity

The second part of your compass is easier. It's where your good-at's and love-to's intersect. Make a list of everything you are good at. Then make a list of everything you love to do. Where the lists converge is your authentic identity. It's where your talent and desire overlap. This tells you what you should be doing in life.

One of my sons, Brian, has been a fighter pilot for over 20 years. It's what he wanted to do since he was very young; he loves to do it and is great at it.

> *Choose a job you love, and you will never have to work a day in your life.*
> *— Confucius*

He joined the navy right out of college and flew both Tomcats and Super Hornets. Today he teaches others around the world how to fly FA-18s. He is often told by others he has the best job in the world. He never disagrees with them.

The Corporate Compass

The corporate compass guides the organization for better or worse, for richer, for poorer, in sickness and in health. It is a core ideology, composed of the company's principles and gifts. The organization's principles must be an honest extension of your personal compass. A leader's compass creates the organization's culture. It determines the choices everyone makes every day (Covey, Merrill, and Merrill).

Why is our company in business? What is our purpose? Just as we have a personal reason for living, a company also has a reason for being. In many cases, it's the same as the company's vision and mission.

Merck	Preserving and improving human life.
Boeing	Being on the leading edge of aviation.
Starbucks	"It has always been, and always will be, about quality. We're passionate about ethically sourcing the finest coffee beans, roasting them with great care, and improving the lives of people who grow them. We care deeply about all of this; our work is never done" (starbucks.com).

Gainesville Health and Fitness	Creating an experience that helps people to get the most out of life while inspiring them to become their best.

An organization's gifts, its core competencies, parallel your personal authentic identity. The core competency is something the business does well and is leveraged throughout the entire organization. What does your company do better than anyone else in the world? Or at least better than any competitor?

Target has core competencies of superior customer care and clean facilities. Walmart has low prices. Disney World has "the show," themed attractions, and employees committed to friendliness.

Compass Summary

You can't run away from your reason for being; you should run toward your identity. Your compass can't be changed easily, so you might as well find it. When both your personal life and your business life are in tune with each other, the results are natural enthusiasm, faith in where you are going, and true happiness.

Crystal Ball Gazing

The rearview mirror is always clearer than the windshield.

— Warren Buffett

Look into the future as best you can. First, let's state the obvious. Most things are beyond our prediction, especially the farther out our gaze. But, as with all things, we can make a best guess. In fact, that's all we can do. Sure, the guess might be wrong, but we must still imagine what is beyond the windshield. We can predict some things that are more likely to occur than others.

I have no apprehension about telling my students there are only three ways out of our country's debt. (1) Lower our standard of living about one-third for a generation, with wages that don't keep up with inflation, higher taxes, and fewer services (all of this is going on as I write). (2) Sell assets. Here, China, we'll sell you San Francisco for a trillion and throw in California for free. (3) Declare bankruptcy. We have all the missiles. What's anyone going to do to us?

A useful way of gazing is "what if" testing. Instead of trying to predict what will happen, it's more about saying, "If XYZ happens, what in turn happens to our culture, staff morale, balance sheet, income statement, etc." Then narrow it down to "Well, X is more likely than Y, and Y is more likely than Z."

> *The future is hard but not impossible to predict. — Andy Redleaf, CEO of the $4 billion hedge fund Whitebox Advisors (he chose this name, as opposed to blackbox, to let everyone know his operation is transparent)*

Before we can figure out what we must do today, we need to see what might happen tomorrow. Then at least we can try to control what happens, as opposed to blindly leaving it to chance.

The future arises from the many things we can't control, such as changing customer tastes. Cisco studies its customers' changing needs and tastes. Once it discerns a change in what customers want, it makes market predictions based on what it sees. Walmart is famous for its customer data mining and data warehousing. Boeing sees rising fuel prices. It positions itself by investing heavily in the Dreamliner, an aircraft made completely out of composite materials, reducing the weight and therefore the fuel cost by 20%. Intel practices a principle of marketing known as time pacing, which means the company anticipates change. As a new product is in production, Dan Rosenblatt notes, Intel managers are working on the next version of it. Richard Schulze, founder of Best Buy, gazed constantly and was able to predict growth in home appliances, musical instruments, and auto maintenance.

Of course, not all gazes are correct. Consider Pepsi and Coke with their Crystal Pepsi and New Coke formulas.

What was my personal look into the future for this book? I see leaders needing to make timely decisions, faced with a flood of data, in an increasingly uncertain world. This is where lots and lots of "what if" testing comes in. If you've already determined which effects X, Y, and Z are likely to have on your company, it's easier to respond to those events as they occur. Given my prediction, I wanted to find a way to help leaders make better decisions than they would make on their own. I tried to do that by examining and reporting how world-class leaders have gone and continue to go about making critical decisions.

You might be asking, "But what happens if you don't have the resources of a Cisco or Walmart?" Almost every business has some association to which it belongs. You should demand that your association finds the best futuristic thinkers in the world, and at every convention and on its website they should present which conditions they think will occur with regard to each of the following uncontrollables:

Competition	Taxes
Technology	Culture
Laws	Customs
Changing consumer tastes	Politics
Changing demographics	Government
Weather	Economy

When I say find the best futurists, I don't mean the ones in the media. Most media-friendly experts tend to have one whopper of an idea and then apply that thought to form all sorts of non-relevant predictions. The best are those who have a good track record, who use many forms of modeling, who understand "the trend is your friend," and who recognize they won't always be right. The more assured a futurist is, the more you should rely on your own predictions.

Futurists aren't much good at predicting impacts, but they are better than average at predicting conditions. Again, categorize and prioritize to determine which you and your stakeholders believe will have the most impact on your business and what those impacts will be.

Foresight, though difficult, is key to market success. Drucker: "Trying to predict the future is like trying to drive down a country road at night with no lights while looking out the back window." Conditions always change, so polish your crystal ball often. What does the future require your company to be?

Denny Klein, CEO of Hydrogen Technology Applications, has invented Aqugen. It's a combustible gas generated from water by using electrolysis. It can power an engine using water. At the time of writing, it is being used in prototype automobiles, and if successful it will be an environmentally friendly supplement to fossil fuels.

Vision

What would you do with your life and your business if you knew you couldn't fail? To achieve the unthinkable, you must first think the unthinkable. Your personal vision is a reflection of your soul. Your company's vision is a reflection of the company's soul. Koo Bon-joon, CEO of LG Electronics, reinforces his vision of being the market leader with his greeting "Let's be number one" and on his business card with "First place company."

> *Good business leaders create a vision, articulate the vision, passionately own the vision, and relentlessly drive it to completion.* — Jack Welch, chairman of General Electric

A traditional way of defining a vision is an ambitious view of the future that everyone in the organization can believe in and that is not readily attainable yet offers a future that is better in important ways than what now exists (Hamel and Prahalad).

My take is a little different. I view vision as the connection between the compass and future opportunities. It's the combination of two components: what you can see in the future and who you are. Is this really possible? Absolutely. Is it exact? Absolutely not. Before you can create a reality, you must create a dream. The dream first appears when you connect your compass with what you see in the future. And, when they are connected, the result is a belief, not a wish.

> *The very essence of leadership is that you have to have a vision.*
>
> *You can't blow an uncertain trumpet.*
>
> — *Theodore Hensburg, president of the University of Notre Dame*

You are bound to see numerous possibilities. Which ones seem to have the greatest potential? Which can contribute the greatest good? Which one will be the most fun? Which ones offer the greatest gap between what is and what can be? Which are most likely to take place? Which will cause your friends to say, "Are you joking?" We need to not just push the envelope but also make it bigger.

> *The phrase "push the envelope" relates to high-speed aircraft performance in dog fighting. There is a diagram that takes into account energy, maneuverability, airspeed, how many G's the pilot needs to make a particular turn, and the turn radius. The graph shows the aircraft's operational capabilities, and the borders are known as the envelope. If you go beyond the envelope in one direction, the plane will stall; in another direction, you can overstress the aircraft or the pilot or both. Good pilots know where they can safely operate within the envelope. Great pilots operate at the edge of the envelope to maximize an aircraft's abilities. Brian Swayne: "I do this in every engagement. To win a fight, you need to be uber-aggressive. Right from the get go I take it to the envelope, bring it back, then back to the edge. This type of flying intimidates the opponent and should advertise this is not the pilot you want to mess with."*

Every once in a while a student who has listened to a more practical teacher in another course asks, "Shouldn't the vision be more realistic?" I then ask the student to go to the nearest wall and reach his fingers as high as he can. Then I ask him to reach even higher. And 100% of the time he can. This illustrates the concept of everyone being able to reach farther than he thinks he can and that any organization's vision should make everyone stretch.

Your dream won't materialize simply by dreaming. It has to be believed by you and your people. It will then take a lot of energy and hard work by both you and your staff. Powell: "Endeavors succeed or fail because of the people involved. Only by attracting the best, the brightest, the most creative people will you accomplish great deeds. Surround yourself with people who take their work seriously, but not themselves, those who work hard and play hard."

Now comes a tricky part. You have to paint the picture of your belief. One of an ambitious, uplifting adventure, more than what has been accomplished in the past, of where the business is going. It is a portrait in which all those in the organization can see themselves fitting. This is speaking in tongues. Not in the biblical sense of different languages but saying something with such energy that everyone understands. We try to bring everyone on board. No fair just painting the picture once. It must be painted over and over and over so that everyone knows not just what the company is doing but also, more importantly, why it is doing it. Mountain climbers go farther on a sunny day than they do on a cloudy one. Why? Because they can see where they're going. Help your people see where they are going.

When Cassius Clay was 12, he told his mom he would be champion of the world. He envisioned himself as the best. He never saw anything else. Positive thinking, hard work, and natural ability allowed Ali to rise to the top.

John Stuart Mill, at age seven, saw himself becoming the greatest philosopher ever. By that age, he had mastered Greek and was studying Latin. Completely self-taught, he studied every day and by the age of 12 had completed, in today's terms, a college education.

Yo-Yo Ma at the age of four knew he would be a string prodigy. At the age of five, he performed the cello for JFK and Eisenhower. He has since created original music as artistic director of the Silk Road Ensemble.

In 1968, Bill Gates used his first computer. It was the spark of an obsession. His dream was to have a computer in every home.

The organization's vision is primarily for you and your staff but not something you'd mind if your other stakeholders saw it. Here are some companies' visions.

McDonald's	To be the world's best quick service restaurant experience. Being the best means providing outstanding quality, service, cleanliness, and value so that we make every customer in every restaurant smile.
Budweiser	Through all of our products, services and relationships, we will add to life's enjoyment.
Amazon	Be the earth's most customer centric company; to build a place where people can come to find and discover anything they might want to buy online.
Heinz	The world's premier food company, offering nutritious, superior tasting foods to people everywhere.
Mattel	To be the premier toy brands — today and tomorrow.

The painter thinks and thinks about his subject before, during, and after he paints his picture. Not only do you need to think about and examine yourself to find your inner compass, but you also need to take that thought, that dream, and plan it, just like a painter does a rough sketch first. Then, as you travel toward your vision, just like the painter, you make subtle changes along the way. With time, the picture becomes more clear.

> *You can't get people excited, unless you can help them see and feel the impact. — Bill Gates*

> *I am talking about a gung-ho attitude that says "we can change things here, we can achieve some awesome goals, we can be the best."*
> *— Colin Powell*

We become what we think about the most. This is a simple but profound truth. When you create your vision and get everyone involved in that picture, some things automatically start to happen. Minds automatically filter out information that doesn't fit with the vision and search for information that does. Individuals associate with those who match the vision and avoid those who don't. Once the artist gets into the middle of his planning, sketching, and painting, things start to align. Anyone studying a painting eventually becomes one with the painter. Anything out of place becomes more evident to both the painter and his audience (Huinker).

The more the picture is reinforced, the more you and your organization move toward it. With time, the more you can pull people into the picture, the more they will pull each other in, and in turn the more optimistic the organization becomes. The hard work starts to be done by one and all of the bees. When the hive knows where they are going, they instinctively know where to apply resources.

Some visions include part of the compass. Some visions are blurred; some are precise. If yours is not yet clear, it will become more concrete as we flow through the rest of the model.

Notice we are doing two things. First, we are continually attempting to look into the future and then apply our perceived strengths to achieve a competitive advantage. Second, we are providing the environment in which to attain a vision. Powell: "Leadership is the art of accomplishing more than the science of management says is possible."

If your mind can conceive, and your heart believe, then you can achieve.

The vision should be something that everyone strives for, but it should remain unfinished. Your organization never wants to ask Peggy Lee's question, "Is that all there is?"

Your compass, both personal and company, will not change much over your lifetime. What you see in the future will change constantly. For that reason, most great companies review their visions at least annually. GM, Chrysler, and Phillip Morris were forced to change their visions. Las Vegas tried to become more family friendly. Cabela's went from a mail order catalog company to more store based.

You might think there is a roadmap for strategic thinking. However, there is only the guiding glow of a lighthouse beacon. We are about to discuss two distinct ways to get you safely into the harbor. Either course will take you to better places. One, a more difficult path, turns out to be the best.

We all know that a trip of a thousand miles must begin with a first step. Left foot in front of right foot. The *incremental approach* is the most common method of obtaining a vision. We take small steps toward continuous improvement. We constantly raise the bar, a little at a time, moving toward our vision. This works. Eric Seidel, winner of eight bracelets: "Become a pro in an incremental sort of way. Take it one step at a time."

Or you can make a leap. I ask my students, "When Jack Nicklaus stepped up to the tee, what do you think went through his mind?" Everyone says something along the line "He visualized his swing" or "He saw the ball going down the fairway." Wrong. Nicklaus saw the ball going into the hole. Then he saw his putt, then his approach shot. Back to his tee shot. He began with the end in mind, and then he figured out what he needed to do to get there.

You can use the *Nicklaus leap*. It's done by constantly emphasizing what the vision is and then empowering your staff to figure out how to reach it. The result is more chaotic than the incremental approach, but when it works it results in greater gains in less time.

Jim Collins, co-author with Jerry Porass of *Built to Last*, relates a discussion with David Packard. "When asked to name the most important product decisions contributing to Hewlett-Packard's remarkable growth rate, he answered entirely in terms of the attributes of the Hewlett-Packard organization." It is the concept of using what a company stands for as the anchor rather than relying on a product. In *Built to Last*, they make the credible points that this approach allows the organization to adapt to the environment, take advantage of changing opportunities, and avoid tunnel vision. Their findings indicate the companies that not only last but also prosper, have a passionately held core ideology coupled with a simultaneous culture of continuous experimentation and progress.

Mission

The mission statement provides organized effort. It's a declaration of purpose for the company's existence. It flows from the vision. But where the vision attempts to look into the future for you and your staff, the mission statement usually focuses on where you are today and is for all to see — employees, customers, vendors, community, all stakeholders. Your vision statement describes where you want to be; your mission statement describes how you will get there (Gillman and White).

In some organizations, the vision and mission are identical or almost so. That might not fit the theory that says the mission is derived from the vision, but it certainly might fit the business's reality.

I always ask my class, "Who works for a business that has a mission statement?" A few hands go up. Then I ask each of the hands what the mission statement is. Few, if any, know. I then ask them if they can tell me the mission statement of the University of Wisconsin. No one knows. If ever there was a mission statement designed by a committee, trying to satisfy everyone, and getting through to no one, this is it.

> The mission of the University of Wisconsin is to develop human resources; to discover and disseminate knowledge; to extend knowledge and its application beyond the boundaries of its campuses; and to serve and stimulate society by developing in students heightened intellectual, cultural, and human sensitivities as well as scientific, professional, and technological expertise and a sense of purpose. Inherent in this broad mission are methods of instruction, research, extended education and public service designed to educate people and improve the human condition. Basic to every purpose of the system is the search for the truth.

The University of Wisconsin–La Crosse is one of many campuses in the UW system. I ask the students if they know the UW-L's mission statement. Of course they don't know it. The faculty don't know it.

> The University of Wisconsin–La Crosse provides a challenging, dynamic, and diverse learning environment in which the entire university community

is fully engaged in supporting student success. Grounded in the liberal arts, University of Wisconsin–La Crosse fosters curiosity and life-long learning through collaboration, innovation, and the discovery and dissemination of new knowledge. Acknowledging and respecting the contributions of all, University of Wisconsin–La Crosse is a regional academic and cultural center that prepares students to take their place in a constantly changing world community.

Zzzzzzzzzzzzzzzzzzzzz.

Although the traditional mission statement broadly describes an organization's present capabilities, customer focus, activities, driving force, products, and so on, here's what I have found to be the most effective. It must be simple, short, easily understood, repeated every day and everywhere. Your mission statement should be so memorable that every employee could spit it out even if someone had a gun to his head (Widuch). It must be simple, inspiring, life affirming (Sinek).

Let's take a look at Big Brothers/Big Sisters.

To make a positive difference in the lives of children and youth, primarily through a professionally supported, one to one relationship with a caring adult, and to assist them in achieving their highest potential as they grow to become confident, competent, and caring individuals, by providing committed volunteers, national leadership, and standards of excellence.

This mission statement covers the purpose, the business, and the values. The problem is it's too long to be memorable. I'd prefer something everyone could recall, such as "To make a positive difference in the lives of children."

How about the Elephant Sanctuary? "A natural-habitat refuge where sick, old and needy elephants can once again walk the earth in peace and dignity." I'd make it even shorter: "A peaceful place for elephants."

Here is my personal one for this book: to help leaders make better decisions than they would have made on their own.

And here are some great mission statements. Some are identical to the companies' visions.

Google	To make the world's information universally accessible and useful.
Microsoft	To help people and businesses throughout the world realize their full potential.
Mayo Clinic	Provide the best care to every patient every day through integrated clinical practice, education, and research.
Harley-Davidson	Fulfill dreams through the experience of motorcycling.
Amazon	To build a place where people can come to find and discover anything they might want to buy online.
Gainesville Health and Fitness	To make Gainesville the healthiest community in America one person at a time, one business at a time.

I certainly agree that the mission statement should be supplemented with the pillars, the clarifying values that hold up the statement. "Home Depot is in the home improvement business, and our goal is to provide the highest level of service, the broadest selection of products, and the most competitive prices." Once the mission is defined, it can be expanded with pillars.

We are a values driven company, and our eight core values include the following:

1. Excellent customer service.
2. Taking care of our people.
3. Giving back.
4. Doing the right thing.
5. Creating shareholder value.
6. Respect for all people.
7. Entrepreneurial spirit.
8. Building strong relationships.

Home Depot then goes on to describe what it means by each of its core values.

Your crystal ball will change, causing an adjustment to your strategic vision that will in turn cause your mission statement to change. Re-evaluate your mission statement every year.

When Gainesville was declared the healthiest community in the United States, Cirulli changed his company's mission to "To keep

Gainesville the healthiest community in America one person at a time, one business at a time."

Howard Schultz, CEO of Starbucks, changed the mermaid logo as a signal that he was going into the energy bar, tea, and cake business and that those Starbucks branded products were going to be available at your local grocery store (Horovitz).

David McConnell in the late 1800s sold books door to door. To get female customers, he gave away small bottles of perfume. The perfume became more popular than his books. Eventually, his company became Avon.

In 1923, the Hassenfeld brothers sold leftover textiles. Then they shifted to making pencils and school supplies. In 1952, they made Mr. Potato Head, and Hasbro was on its way.

Apple used to be in computers and was flat-lining. Then the iPod, the iPhone, and the iPad made it into a parabolic stock. Apple has reinvented itself from a computer company to a device company, solving customers' needs in many areas of their lives.

Xerox redefined itself from producing office equipment such as copiers and printers to better serving its clients by providing extensive customer support services (Rosenblatt).

How do visions and missions compare? With those below, you can see how some missions flow from visions and how some are essentially, or actually, the same.

Hellmuth	*Vision*: To become the best poker player in the world.
	Mission: To become the best poker player in the world.
Disney	*Vision*: Bring happiness to millions.
	Mission: Create happiness by providing the finest in entertainment for people of all ages, everywhere.
Coca-Cola	*Vision*: A Coke within arm's reach of everyone on the planet.
	Mission: To refresh the world . . . in body, mind, and spirit (Lussier).
Nike	*Vision*: To bring inspiration and innovation to every athlete in the world.

Mission: To bring inspiration and innovation to every athlete in the world.

So far we have used mostly the right side of the brain, where we can imagine and dream. In the next step, strategic planning, we go to the left side, where we start to probe and analyze.

Strategic Planning/Execution

Before we go through strategic planning and execution, let's review what thought leader and author Simon Sinek says: "There are leaders and there are those who lead. Leaders hold a position of power or authority. Those who lead inspire us. We follow those who lead not because we have to, but because we want to." Sinek has found that inspirational leaders constantly tell everyone "why" they are doing something, not what they are doing or how they are doing it. The "why" is your compass, vision, and purpose. When you tell everyone your compass, your vision, your purpose, your belief, you constantly attract employees, customers, and stakeholders who agree with your "why." If you and I believe the same thing, an emotional bond is built. We share a common cause. Jerry Noyce, CEO of Health Fitness: "People want to master their position when their views and the company views align." Trust and loyalty follow. When we have the trust and loyalty of our people, planning and execution flow easily.

Before we try to implement a strategy, we must have these enduring questions answered.

- Why are we?
- Who are we?
- What do we want to become?
- What are we trying to do?

Every time I use the word *strategy*, I state an action or force or where to apply force. The original meaning of strategy is from the military — "to use force" — and force is what we use in business to accomplish things.

As Steve Ballmer, CEO of Microsoft, puts it, Gates' business plan for

Microsoft was "basically an extension of the all-night poker games Bill and I used to play at Harvard" (McManus).

The strategic plan/execution is where we take the vision and mission and turn them into reality or action maps by creating goals, objectives, strategies, and tactics. But plans only get you in the game.

> Vision is nothing without execution.
>
> — Lyle Berman

Here's how best to think of each. There is the "what" and the "how." The goal is the general "what," the objective is the specific "what." The strategy is the general "how," the tactic is the specific "how," and the action maps are what need to be done and who is going to do them. You might find your organization defines its objectives as I define goals, or it might not use the terms "strategy" and "tactics" as I do. Semantics. What's important is covering each as opposed to what each is called.

Strategy should drive structure (Roberto). Once the strategic decision is made, we build or select organizations to execute it.

A *goal* is a general statement of what we want to accomplish, where we want to be (Horwath). It is intangible, abstract. No timeline. In some cases, the goal is the same as the vision or mission.

If you have too many goals, it is difficult to achieve any of them. Tony Petrucciani, CEO of Single Source Systems, set 15 goals for the year. The result was a shortfall of over 10% in sales. He freely admits, "Nobody focused on any one thing." Now he sets fewer goals (Macht). I think the proper number is three but certainly no more than five. A few examples follow.

- Become the pre-eminent drug maker worldwide.
- Bring happiness to millions.
- Make information available all over the world.

Setting goal priorities cannot be underestimated. Your priority becomes a dominating thought and consumes the majority of your and your staff's conscious and unconscious efforts, to the detriment of any other goal. Consider this. When Jobs was ousted from Apple, he had a philosophy of making a great product and making a profit. Apple declined, and he was brought back in. He discovered that the philosophy had changed to making a profit and a great product. Profit before product. Once he re-established great product before profit, Apple's turnaround began.

When I teach marketing, I disregard the dweeb definition in the text and tell my students that "Marketing is satisfying customer needs at a profit." Note that it is not making a profit by satisfying customer needs. Customer before profit. In great companies, profit is a result of, not a reason for. Goal priorities matter.

An *objective* turns the goal into what we want to accomplish specifically (Horwath). What gets measured gets done, and an objective is a precise target. It is tangible, concrete, with time-specific metrics.

- Have a 20% world market share within five years.
- Serve 30 million customers a year.
- Make information available in over 100 languages within a year.

A *strategy* is a general statement of applying force to accomplish the objective (Horwath). Sometimes there is only one strategy; other times several are needed. Strategies can include resources needed, skills to develop, or knowledge to acquire. At this point in the process, they aren't difficult; in fact, they are surprisingly easy to figure out.

- Commit massive amounts of research and development for new products.
- Build properties that will bring happiness to our guests.
- Hire the best people who can translate information.

A strategy is usually the first indication of how we are going to allocate our resources. Since there are always limits, we must be careful how we allocate our time, talent, and treasure.

> *Tactics without strategy is the noise before defeat.* — *Sun Tzu*

A *tactic* is the specific way we apply force to accomplish the objective (Horwath). Usually, several tactics are employed for each strategy. Often a tactic introduces or reinforces a timeline.

- R & D is to spend $2 billion in the next three years to create no fewer than 20 new products.
- The CFO is to obtain equity financing for $300 million for our chief of development to build two new properties within the next four years.
- Human Resources is to spend whatever it takes to hire the world's top 100 language translators within the next three months.

Action maps are the specific things that need doing and who is going to do them. Quarterly, monthly, weekly, daily to-do lists. Details. Activities. All the things that must happen to execute the tactics. Cumulative tactics and action maps are the treads on the strategic plan tank. How long will it take? When will it be done? For every tactic, there are numerous action maps. Although nicely laid out, they are fluid, often changing daily or even hourly.

Contained and perhaps repeated somewhere in the objective, strategy, or tactic is a time element (usually the date it must be completed or in some cases the amount of time to be spent), the target metrics to be used to measure success, and often the person responsible. If your ground forces — those who really do the work — haven't been involved until now, this is where they take over. They are the ones who bring the action maps to life.

Strategic planning and execution are designed to answer the following questions.

- What's the objective?
- Who is responsible?
- When will it be done?

Figure 2.2 illustrates strategic planning. Please review the Strategic-Thinking model at the start of this chapter (Figure 2.1, page 30). Also recall the discussion about bricks and the house. We talked about the university just giving you the bricks rather than the house. This model contains both bricks and parts of the house. Notice that the base of the Strategic-Thinking model is your compass — something very general. At the top of the model, everything becomes specific. The strategic-planning portion starts with the general (goal) and ends with specifics (tactics and action maps).

Figure 2.3 illustrates the true complexity of strategic thinking. It becomes even more complex as you fold in the knowledge components and the Decision-Making model we will cover in the next few chapters.

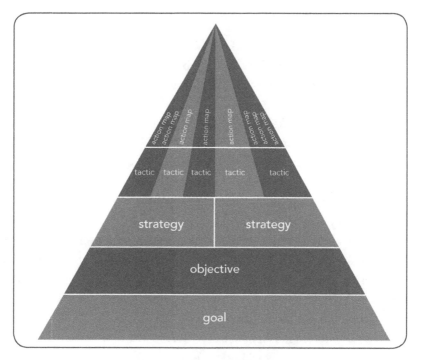

Figure 2.2 Strategic Planning

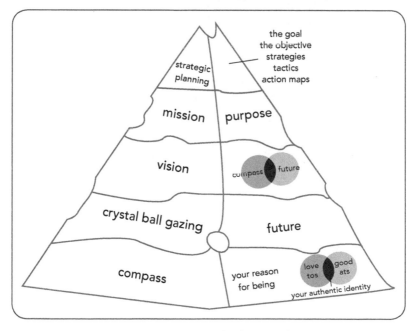

Figure 2.3 Strategic-Thinking Reality

Stakeholder Involvement

In the chapter on decision making, we will discuss the importance of stakeholder involvement. The same can be said for the Strategic-Thinking model. Allow stakeholders in on your strategic thinking. The earlier they are involved, the better.

Our children are stakeholders. As they were growing up, sometimes we played the Christmas envelope game. I wish we'd done this every year. On Christmas Eve, our children, in front of their siblings, would tell Carol and me what they wanted to do with their lives. Then they'd write down what they'd do over the next year to get there. Whatever they wrote would be put into envelopes with their names on them and sealed. The next Christmas Eve they would again state what they planned to do with their lives, and they were free to change their plans whenever they wished. If their visions hadn't changed (surprisingly, none ever changed), they would open up their envelopes from the previous year and read aloud their plans. Then they'd say whether they had accomplished what they said they'd do. If Brian had said he was going to read eight books on aviation, he proudly said he'd read 12. If Chuck had said he would practice 100,000 serves, he'd made sure he did over 300 a day (I didn't allow him to practice on Sundays). Although we were the leaders, we didn't tell Chuck and Brian which careers they had to pursue. Each child was allowed to create his own compass, vision, mission, goals, objectives, strategies, tactics, and action maps. And when that happens, especially in front of peers, they push themselves harder than we could ever have pushed them. Chuck played on the professional tennis tour. Brian became a Tomcat pilot.

> *Nothing that is worth knowing can be taught.* — *Oscar Wilde*

The same process is often used in sales organizations. First each salesperson forecasts what he thinks would be a realistic stretch (i.e., the objective) for the company's sales within a specified period of time. A committee made up of the CEO, the sales manager, and the top salespeople then review the inputs and arrive at an objective. Each salesperson is then allowed to review the objective and how it was determined. Then each salesperson sets his own quota. Those who buy into the objective, and set their own tar-

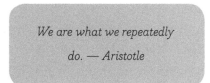

We are what we repeatedly do. — Aristotle

gets, will drive themselves harder than their bosses ever could.

Stakeholders should be involved as early as possible, but at a minimum allow your stakeholders to be involved from the start of the strategic-planning process. If they help to set the goal, they will figure out their own objectives (usually more ambitious than you might have), strategies, tactics, and action maps.

The more you do anything, the easier it becomes. The more we use both sides of the brain, the more natural we connect emotion and analysis (Gilkey, Caceda, and Kilts). You can have the will, but to execute well you need experience. Time, focus, and experience are needed to learn how to think strategically without effort.

Every failure is a blessing in disguise, providing it teaches some needed lesson one could not have learned without it. — Napoleon Hill

Riding a bicycle isn't natural. We get on first with training wheels. The training wheels then come off, and a parent holds the bike as we try to gain balance. We fall and fall again. Through experience, we learn to ride. And now, when we get on a bike, we don't even think about it. We do everything we need to without conscious thought.

A man who carries a cat by the tail learns something he can learn in no other way. — Mark Twain

Superior poker players are constantly internalizing their Sinek why and their vision (Hellmuth's becoming the best). With their actions and clear, concise, consistent rhetoric, superior organizational leaders go a step further and create a distinctive internal brand and corporate culture by constantly reinforcing the company's why and vision.

If you haven't used this Strategic-Thinking model much, play tight, wait for a solid opportunity. As you use it over and over, and become proficient, you'll gain more experience and confidence.

> *The general who wins the battle makes many calculations in his temple before the battle is fought.* — *Sun Tzu*

3

Knowledge

The more you know, the less you fear.

Making Decisions

Leaders make decisions. You are the handle of a whip. The handle wiggles a little, those at the end of the whip are violently moved. Your decisions will never be perfect, but they should be the wisest possible.

A good decision is not one that necessarily has a good outcome but one that was based on sound analysis at the time it was made. Cardoza: "It's not a mistake if you made the correct decision with the information available even if the outcome is not favorable."

> *The more information you have, the better decisions you make.*
>
> — *Joe Gow*

A poor decision might result in a good outcome, but that doesn't make it a good decision. One of the worst things that can happen is you play poor cards out of position and win. Then you think you are God's gift to the poker world and do it again. And again. Until you lose all your chips. Your Sham-Wow is a hit. So you throw all of your profits into what? Does anyone remember the next product?

> *Institutional investors spend a lot of money on information.*
>
> — *Andy Redleaf*

There are three stages to go through in making a judicious decision. It will seldom be the best, because in life you hardly ever know if it was the best. But, by using this process, you can be confident that you have made the most intelligent decision with the information available at the time.

First, you must gain some knowledge, and that knowledge needs to be organized in a specific manner. You need to know the following.

- Yourself
- Your competitors
- Your stakeholders
- The uncontrollables
- The game

It's a building process, as shown in Figure 3.1.

Second, after you have some basic knowledge, you must ask many more questions and get many more answers.

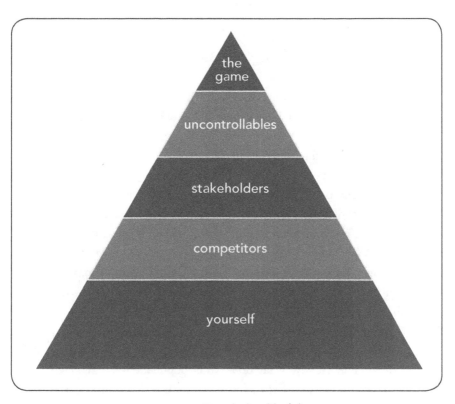

Figure 3.1 Knowledge Model

And third, use a logical Decision-Making model.

This appears pretty simple, but it's not easy. Each section, each paragraph, should seem straightforward or at least understandable. But putting it all together isn't easy. In fact, it's presumptuous to think anyone can do it flawlessly.

Eventually, you will have a sudden flash of insight, an "aha" moment. You will get it. It might be during one of the chapters. It might be at the end of the book. It might be during your third or fourth reading. Or it might be several months from now. When you have your epiphany, your "aha," you'll understand that no one can see the whole at a glance, no one's decisions are spot on, and nothing is definitive, but you'll see that you can get your mind around much more than you used to, more than most of your competitors. You will gain an advantage and be able to make the wisest possible decision.

Data, 411, and Knowledge

Money flows clockwise on the poker table — that is, to those who have more information.

There are the cards on the board. There are the bets, calls, and folds. All in plain view. That's public information. Available to you and your competitors for interpretation. In business, there is a lot of information available, but it often requires digging to find it.

Bill Gates: "In poker, a player collects different pieces of information — who's betting boldly, what cards are showing, what this guy's pattern of betting and bluffing is — and then crunches all that data together to devise a plan for his own hand. I got pretty good at this kind of information processing" (McManus). Eisenhower was "a great poker player, . . . a tremendous man for analyzing the other fellow's mind, what options are open to the other fellow, and what line he can best take to capitalize or exploit the possibilities" (McManus).

Then there are your hole cards and your opponents' hole cards. Proprietary information. That's what is really critical. What do you hold? Much more importantly, what does your opponent hold? The greatest poker players in the world are concerned more with the strength of their opponents' cards and the situation than with the strength of their own. Phil Gordon, Netsys executive, finisher at several WSOP final tables, and poker author: "The cards are immaterial. The situation is much more important. If you know what your opponent has, it doesn't matter what you have."

Data aren't useful information. Today business data are measured in zettabytes: that's a trillion gigabytes. Data are sound without music. Raw data are noise. It's like trying to get a drink from a fire hose. The information must be sifted through and massaged to become useful. The more information gathered, the more time it takes and the more difficult it is to discern critical knowledge from unimportant information. The best decisions are made by those who have the most useful information.

I get a lot of information but can quickly figure out which are the two or three things that are most important. — Lyle Berman

> *The most important commodity I know is information.*
>
> — *Gordon Gekko*

Although I will use the words *information* and *knowledge* interchangeably, please understand that knowledge is information placed in the context of an opportunity or a problem. Knowledge is power in poker and in business. You must have knowledge to lead, and the more of it you have the easier it is to lead.

80/20

In the early 1900s, Vilfredo Pareto noticed that 80% of the Italian land was owned by 20% of the people. He also observed that about 20% of the peapods in his garden contained about 80% of the peas. He came up with the 80/20 rule. It means that most of the important effects come from a few of the causes.

Most of a professional poker player's winnings don't come from other professionals. The money comes from those rich businessmen who don't know the game nearly as well as they think they do (males think they are better looking than they are and think their poker skill is better than it is). Gordon: "You are going to win 90% of your money from the worst three players at the table. Target the weak players." When targeting a weak player, the best will isolate him, bet regardless of what he has, and keep raising until getting pushed back.

You can't be an expert in everything. You have to decide which areas to focus on. In the previous section, we discussed information. Concentrate on the 20% of the information you think most important, and turn that 20% into as much usable knowledge as possible. Which uncontrollables will probably have the greatest impact on your future? If you can list 10, study the top two carefully.

Covey's Fire Within

The greatest explorer on this earth never takes voyages as long as those of the man who descends to the depth of his heart. — *Julien Green*

There are four parts to knowing yourself. Steven Covey's model illustrates the Fire Within, where your spiritual, mental, social, and physical selves overlap (Figure 3.2).

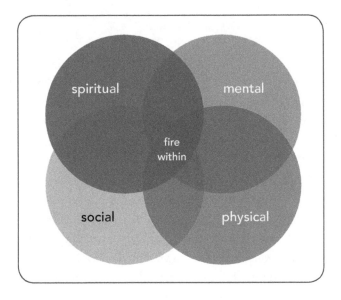

Figure 3.2 Covey's Fire Within Model

I have found that reality is skewed somewhat: that is, for most leaders, their spiritual foundation dominates everything else (Figure 3.3).

You'll see, as we examine each segment, how something in one circle can apply in another. As with all things human, there are few true edges to any circle.

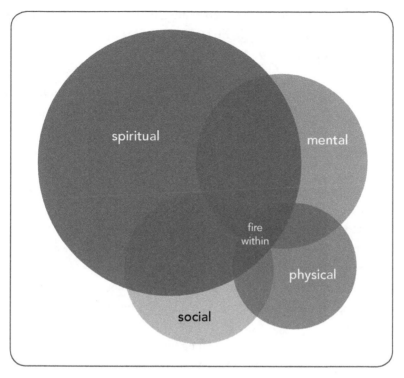

Figure 3.3 The Fire Within Reality

Your Spiritual Self

When I wrote earlier about your compass, I debated whether to include it here or as part of the Strategic-Thinking model. Obviously, I ended up putting it in as part of the chapter on strategic thinking. It just as easily could have been placed here since it is your spiritual essence.

The point of the compass is to discover who you are inside and then learn to live true to your core. We can try to disguise ourselves as something we are not, but eventually our true selves are revealed, especially in high-pressure situations.

Truth withstands every test. It fears no trial. If people don't trust you, your decision-making ability, the decisions you make, and any leadership qualities you possess are worthless.

Lou Holtz was asked how he attracted and kept talent; he said there were three questions he always tried to answer yes to. Can I trust you? Do you really care about me? Are you committed to excellence? What a perfect three-legged stool to start with. He also said trust is by far the most important. Without it, the last two mean little. I agree.

> *Leadership is based on truth and character. — Vince Lombardi*

Brian Tracy: "Listening builds trust." Careful, active listening builds lasting trust.

Trust does not come from an instant meeting. Although most people decide within the first 90 seconds of meeting someone whether or not he is trustworthy, true trust comes from long, enduring relationships. Social media try to bring us together but keep us physically apart. As society becomes faster, with more reliance on technology, less trust is built, because we don't take the time to slowly develop sustained relationships. We are like spouses leaving notes for each other on the fridge because our schedules seldom mesh. Neighborhood dogs know each other better than neighbors know each other.

To emphasize openness and a willingness to listen, Carlos Brito, CEO of Anheuser-Busch doesn't have a private office.

> *We can afford to lose money. We can't afford to lose reputation.*
> *— Warren Buffett*

Bill McAllister, retired CEO of Colonial Mechanical Corporation: "*Always, always* do what you say you're going to do *when* you say you're going to do it."

Guident made a decision not to publicize a defect in some of its defibrillators and waited until deaths occurred before recalling them (O'Toole and Bennis).

> *A dollar is not worth as much as you think it is. Your honesty is worth a lot more. — T. Boone Pickens*

Bill Pearl writes the following.

It happened backstage at the London Palladium a few minutes before the Mr. Universe contest.

The show was billed as "the physique contest of the century." Lots of tension among the contestants. Almost every top bodybuilder in the world was competing. Sergio Olivia, Mr. Olympia, was definitely the favorite.

A young French boy, about seven or eight, accompanied by his father, was backstage watching us warm up. After some prodding by his father, who felt Sergio would be the winner, the boy approached him with a book in hand and waited for a signature.

The boy had made a mistake. He got in Sergio's way. Sergio pushed the boy aside and screamed, "Get out of here. I don't have time for you!" The boy's face dropped. The father's face dropped. They were both devastated.

After awhile the father looked around. He pushed the boy toward me. He slowly walked over, head bowed, autograph book at arm's length, afraid to look me in the eyes.

Not because I'm such a great guy, but because I had seen the despair on the child's face, I signed my name. Then I put the boy on my shoulder. He flexed his skinny little arm while the father took a photograph. I put the boy down, smiled at his dad and said in my best Oregon French, the only French words I knew, "Merci beaucoup." It was all over. It took less than two minutes.

I never saw that child again. But, I did see his father once more. It was an hour later that day during the competition. He was looking at me from the judge's table with a big smile on his face, nodding his head up and down, and saying "Yes . . . yes!"

I did win my fifth Mr. Universe title that day, at the age of 41. By one vote.

Bill's story is not unusual. What goes around really does come around.

Barry Greenstein, acquisition negotiator for Symantec and winner of over $7 million in poker earnings, donates all of his tournament winnings to charity. Mike Sexton wins $1 million and immediately donates $500,000 to charity. They believe you get more than you give. Pickens: "I spend what I need to and give the rest away."

New York's Times Square. Early evening. Cirulli and I were on our way to see *Beauty and the Beast*. We decided to walk from our hotel. We were in a hurry. One of my former students, who was in the cast, had invited us backstage if we could get there early. A heavy rain had just stopped. The sidewalk was still wet. We carefully avoided the puddles since we both had on our best suits. Crowds waited on both sides of the street for the light to turn green so they could rush across.

The light turns. The crowd pushes. An elderly homeless woman falls and hits her head on the curb. Blood spurts. Everyone looks, but no one stops. Except Joe. Joe rushes to help her. Oblivious that his pants are getting soaked in an oily puddle, he takes out his handkerchief to put pressure on her wound. He attends to her as if she were his mother.

I can't forget the pain of my conscience when I didn't stop on my own. I knew I should have. If we really will be judged on how we treat the least of us, I know where Joe will be.

Gates: "My mother never stopped pressing me for doing more for others." Kindness is the only language the blind can see and the deaf can hear. Berman: "The culture I was brought up in was very prone to charitable things. As part of what we do, we give back." The most important things in life are not things.

Do your best to heal wounds of the past. If you don't, you'll find your mind wandering back to hurtful vignettes at the most inopportune times, distracting you from focusing on your vision.

Here's a good story. Four students were doing well in class but decided to go to the Saturday-night football game a few hundred miles away. They slept all day Sunday and still weren't feeling well that Sunday night and decided to see if they could get out of taking the final exam on Monday. They called and said they'd had a flat tire during their trip and asked if they could take the exam on Tuesday. The professor agreed. The next morning they came in to take the exam. The professor put each of the four in a separate room. There were two questions on the final. The first was easy, and it was worth five points. The next question was worth 95 points. It was "Which tire?"

If a person is honest in one part of his life, he is likely to be honest in all parts of his life. I have found I can tell a lot about someone by playing games with him, especially if the game is one on one. Some tennis opponents often call the ball out when clearly it was in. Can you live with yourself? One thing you'll find is that long-term winners, life-long winners, never cheat. Integrity and honor can't be overemphasized.

We're in Wausau, Wisconsin for the men's finals. A big crowd is watching the match. Chuck, age 12, is playing against an adult tennis pro from Chicago. It's a third-set, nine-point tiebreaker.

The first person to score five points wins. The score is 4–4 in the tiebreaker. The next point wins the match and the tournament.

It's call your own lines. This means that, if you don't know if the ball is in or out, you must call it in favor of your opponent.

Chuck's opponent serves a bullet, and Chuck spanks it back. Long baseline rally. The Chicago pro goes for a winner, and the ball lands near Chuck's feet at the baseline. The ball is out by several inches. But, just as the ball hits, Chuck blinks. I see him stare at where he thinks the ball landed and realize he can't tell if the ball was in or out. I know it was out. The crowd knows it was out. Several spectators yell, "Out." Chuck's eyes and mine lock for several seconds. He knows what he has to do.

"Good," he says quietly.

And there is the other end of the spectrum. PCA faced charges that its executives knew its peanuts were tainted but ordered them to be shipped to customers anyway. Reports of excessive moisture (which causes peanut contamination), roasters that didn't heat properly (to destroy germs), insects, and rat droppings fueled the charges. One of the PCA cooks admitted, "I never ate the peanut butter and wouldn't allow my kids to eat it" (Boone and Kurtz).

You are the ethical ceiling in your organization. If you went to work for someone who had lower ethics than you, what would you do? You would leave. That's what will happen to anyone in your business who has higher ethics than you. He will leave. All your staff will have the same or lower ethics than you.

> *Try not to become a man of success but a man of value.* — *Albert Einstein*

Your Mental Self

Following are questions you need to answer truthfully about your mental self. As we discuss them, you'll see that I jump in and out of metaphors related to poker.

- Are you disciplined?
- Are you aggressive?
- Do you know when to become passive?
- Are you trained in the fundamentals?
- Do you make at least one improvement every day?
- Have you developed a great memory?
- Do you understand your own biases?
- Do you know your own leaks?
- Do you go on tilt?
- Do you know where your tipping points are?
- Can you control your fear?
- Can you stand up to the bully?
- Can you play without ever giving up?
- If necessary, can you fight?
- Can you play high stakes?
- Can you learn from your losses, not just your wins?
- Can you learn from others?
- Can you treat disaster as a gift?
- Can you remain positive no matter what?
- Do you care but not too much?
- Do you know if you have superior skill?
- Can you play your A game all the time?
- Have you learned from your failures?
- Who is smarter, more experienced?
- Do you know the f word — fun?

If you know the answers to these questions, you are on your way to a proper mindset.

James McManus, with three final table finishes and author of *Cowboys Full* and *Positively Fifth Street*: "Lying in wait is what good poker players do best." To be successful in anything, we must learn control and patience.

Often you will go card dead. Although this is a usual statistical variation, the table thinks you are a tight wuss, but neither the situation nor the cards allow you to play. The average player becomes bored and plays hands even when he knows he shouldn't. In the long run, patience pays. The tortoise versus the hare.

Patient persistence is important. Many visionary companies didn't have initial success. IRobot, the company that invented and introduced the Roomba Robot Floorvac, failed many times before it came across a product it could sell to the public. During its first eight years in business, it invented over 20 robotic devices. Every one unsuccessful. But it persisted and kept trying until it had a hit (Rosenblatt).

Every manager has faced the situation of being under pressure to hire and choosing between settling and waiting for the right person. Disney had been a year without a COO when CEO Michael Eisner felt the burden of getting someone in to handle the position. He considered Barry Diller and Michael Ovitz. He preferred Diller but chose Ovitz because he thought Diller wouldn't accept the job offer. Conflicts arose. Ovitz lasted only a year (Hanson). Hiring someone because we are too tired of interviewing is not the right play, and we know it is not the right play. Small businesses often hire internally because it is easier, but often it's the wrong move. We must wait until we find the right person. If the product isn't right, keep searching and researching.

You drive home after a few beers with your friends. You know you're buzzed but don't want to call a cab, so you roll the dice and hope you aren't pulled over. You grab a driver instead of a three-iron even though you know it would take a miracle to drive the pond. You call a pot-sized bet with nothing but a gutter because "you might get paid if you catch." Joe Chilsen, turnaround specialist and world-class teacher: "Throw out the anchor and slow down a bit."

There is another discipline that is often overlooked: keeping a daily journal. Most great poker players look back and realize that, as they were learning, they kept detailed records of what time of day they played, what they had to eat, who was at the table, and they tried to draw correlations between what was going on when they won or when they lost. In their diaries, they also kept track of lessons learned and feelings as they increased their insights. Many great leaders do the same. A side benefit of keeping a journal is that, when you look back on what has happened in your life and what you were feeling at the time, it's a window through which you can see your compass.

> *The game favors the bold.*
>
> *— Hugh Shelton, warrior and chairman of the Joint Chiefs of Staff*

The best players blend aggression and assertiveness. These are qualities that either are in their DNA or they have acquired. There is a subtle difference between aggression and assertion. Think of it as two dads disciplining their children. The assertive dad tells the child what he did wrong and why it disappointed him in a clear, concise, and consistent manner. The aggressive father can say the same words but does so in a louder voice and a tone that is more accusatory than consultative (Huinker).

When poker players are in a hand, they play it aggressively. Testosterone helps one to be forceful. Long after the hand, as they analyze their play, they are assertive. The military uses the same process with an "after action review."

> *If you want to win big money in tournament poker, you are going to have to play aggressively. It's simply not a coincidence that all the guys you see on TV are winning millions of dollars. They all have one thing in common, and that's aggression. — Daniel Negreanu*

You will have to fight for lots of tournament pots, especially when you have position or play is shorthanded. As the blinds and antes escalate, during the late stages, you will have no choice but to be more aggressive. The same holds true as your stack dwindles. Aggressive play is mathematically correct when big payouts are skewed to the top finishers, as in televised events (Harrington). Even on draws with 10 or more outs, you'll see the best players bet as though they have a made hand, sometimes three barreling on the river even when they have missed. You won't see many tight, weak calls. Pounce or fold.

I let Tim, an aggressive player, know before class that he will not be allowed to look at his cards during our demonstration and that he is only to decide what to do based on his position and betting patterns of his opponent. In class, I then ask Tim and another student to go outside and shut the door. I explain to the class that Tim will not be able to look at his cards; he is only to fold, bet, call, or raise based on his position and his opponent's betting patterns. I then bring both students back into class and tell them we are going to conduct an experiment on incomplete information. They are going to play heads up. Physically, they will be back to back, and, while each will be able to see the board cards, neither will be able to determine tells, nor will they be able to see showdown cards. Of course, Tim's opponent is allowed to look at his own cards. Seventy percent of the time Tim wins. He does so simply by picking his aggressive spots based entirely on his opponent's betting pattern. The point is, calculated aggression pays.

And it pays in all forms of competition. Brian has a well-worn Tomcat control stick mounted with this inscription: "The man who is aggressive, who pushes the fight is the pilot who is successful in combat and who has the best opportunity for surviving and coming home" (Johnson). In the game of cat and mouse, it's more cat and less mouse.

The aggressive-loose player who always bets when he is in a hand has an advantage. No one knows what he has. The aggressive-loose company that constantly releases products or acquires other companies has the same advantage.

Higher stakes entail more aggression in both poker and business. The businessperson aggressively pursues his vision. It might take the form of aggressively capturing the market, developing a brand, a product, an industry, hiring the best people, attacking a competitor, or any one of several other factors, but in most cases aggression pays off. Top companies tend to invest earlier and more aggressively than their competitors.

When you have and keep the lead, the table reacts to you. Keep the lead and make chasers pay. If you were the first to bet, continue putting pressure on your opponents. If you reraised and were called, when he checks, bet.

If you were first to market with a substantial investment in a new product, continue with another substantial investment. When adopting an aggressive strategy of being the first, you want competitors to fold now. 3M is a company that has been doing this for years.

When Apple goes to market with a new product or new product line, it should follow it up with providing unique services and updates so that it further separates itself from imitators (Rosenblatt).

In tournament play, to maintain your starting stack, you need to win at least one set of blinds and antes per round. But the blinds and antes continue to increase throughout the tournament, so winning just one set of blinds and antes won't allow you to survive. The best players fight to win more than their fair share of blinds and antes.

If players yet to act are weak, even in middle position, you can play as though you have the button. If you wish, you can control the hand.

Even if you have given away what you are willing to settle for in a negotiation, an aggressive play often wins. On the reality show about a pawn shop in Vegas, *Pawn Stars*, you see the old man throw out a price lower than the seller, and when the seller tries to meet him in the middle the old man lowers the price that he was willing to pay. This almost always results in the seller taking the original price he was offered.

A great poker player knows he cannot always be aggressive. Sometimes it's prudent to sit back and be passive. There are times for cautious play. For example, in tournament play, when you go up against another big stack, you run the risk of being knocked out. It's more important to protect your chips rather than your hand. This is especially true if you are out of position or find yourself in a multi-way pot with just a top pair or an overpair. Top pair usually wins small pots but loses big pots. It's awfully easy to fall in love with AK with a K on the flop and get snapped by a set or two pair (Huinker). Passive play is often used when the payout is spread out over a wider field, as with online tournaments.

Passive play in business can be when we continue to do what has proven successful in the past. It is often the least risky option. Do we run the same profitable promotional campaign we did last year or try something new?

Medications and over-the-counter pharmaceuticals play a similar game. With so much competition and so many substitutes, brands such as Aleve shouldn't and don't push too aggressively. They advertise with simple themes such as "That's value. That's Aleve" (Rosenblatt). Banks such as Countrywide, Wachovia, and Bear Sterns, which aggressively pursued sub-prime mortgages or commercial real estate deals in the face of ever-rising land values, all in the name of aggressive growth and profit, are the ones that either failed or were swallowed up into the ever-growing conglomerate banks. With regard to home loans, almost all banks play passively by flipping their loans to the aggressive Fannie and Freddy (Huinker). Samsung is intentionally passive until it is convinced the market is solid and will continue to be strong.

Our competitor has decided to distribute its product nationwide. Do we remain focused on a few outlets (almost a fold), follow its lead (a call), or try to out-distribute it (a raise)? The fold or call might be the better play.

> *Investments are divided between coupon clippers (i.e., cash flow) and security resellers (i.e., those who own things they intend to sell to someone else). We try to be coupon clippers. You don't get paid for taking risks. You get paid for eliminating risks. — Andy Redleaf*

Shoveling manure is fun if you know someday you'll ride the pony. Spend over half of your time improving your fundamentals. It's fundamentals, fundamentals, fundamentals. Practice does not make perfect, perfect practice makes perfect. Pressure and time are the geology of life. Maximum effort = minimum risk.

Once a player has gone through his learning curve, playing 100+ hours per week for several weeks, he then spends numerous hours studying data from his online poker management software, such as Hold'em Manager. More hours on Internet forums such as 2+2 and Poker 5's. He watches videos of other players, he talks with other players about difficult hands. He lives, breathes, and eats poker. This all-or-nothing approach is what separates the greats from the goods.

It's similar to the weekend golfer versus the pro. The best pros spend hours on the range perfecting the shaping of their shots from left to right, right to left. They know exactly how far they can hit with each club at precisely each effort point. In short, they practice all pieces of the game. Not just the game (Huinker).

Fundamental words of advice for beginners. You play too many hands. You chase too much. In business, this translates into focusing on what you do best as opposed to trying to copy your competitors. Many businesses don't even realize they are selling some items at a loss simply because they are afraid to slow down the top-line sales figures. The most fundamental part of business is to produce a product or service and sell it for more than it costs you to put it together. Only then can a business move on to more sophisticated "plays." For those starting off in business, find what you do best and stick to it — your corporate compass.

> *Do what you are good at. Let someone else do the other things. — Joe Chilsen*

Another tried-and-true business basic. Bill McAllister: "Pay for top talent, even if you think you can't afford it. You can't afford not to have top talent. Be honest about your own strengths and weaknesses. Then delegate in clear terms. Don't hover. Stay out of the way." Focus on exploiting your strengths as opposed to compensating for your weaknesses.

The progression for poker fundamentals runs something like this.

- Knowing who you are
- Values, vision, mission — your personal compass
- Vocabulary and language
- Rules

- History
- Opponents
- Strategies depending on rules
- Discipline
- Tight starting hands
- Position
- Stack size
- Bet sizing
- Pot odds
- Implied odds
- Deception
- Betting patterns
- Memory games
- Aggression
- Looser starting hands
- Strategies depending on opponents and situation

The progression for business fundamentals, though not usually followed in business school, is not dissimilar.

- Knowing who you are
- Values, vision, mission — your corporate compass
- Vocabulary and language
- History
- Basic economic and other rules
- Stakeholders
- Competitors
- Finances
- Strategies depending on rules
- A few new products with potential
- Probabilities
- Aggression
- Several new products, risky, but with breakout potential
- Strategies depending on stakeholders/competitors and situation

The dictionary is the only place where "success" comes before "work." You do not rise to the occasion, you fall back on your training. Sully was able to land his plane on the Hudson River because he went to the Air Force Academy. I'm sure its pilots had the same training Brian did. They practiced, over and over, a flame out. What's a flame out? The pilot turns off his engine above the airfield and then must land the plane without turning the engine back on. Brian had hours of training designed to help him react instantly to unforeseen situations.

We taxied onto the carrier's catapult in the blackness of night with only the soft yellow lights of the taxi directors to guide us. I reviewed my instruments through the night filters the crew had just installed to eliminate the glare. On the catapult, in tension, running up the engines, everything looked good. The exterior lights, the signal to the deck, came on, and we were ready for launch. Seven seconds later it happened.

We had a good cat shot, but the snap of the catapult popped off one of the filters. It fell towards the cockpit floor. The instrument it had been filtering blinded me, and it took my eyes a good three seconds to adjust. Three seconds can be a lifetime in a Tomcat, especially at a low altitude. Fez and I were hot mike, so when the filter came off I said, "Oh, oh!" Not what the man in the back seat who has no control over the F-14 wants to hear. The boss on the carrier is yelling, "Climb off the cat." Fez is screaming, "Burner, burner!" I am totally overwhelmed.

I plug in the burners at about the same time my eyes are adjusting and see a flat fly-away attitude. In fact, we have been flying at a level of just a few feet off the water since the cat shot. When I tried to rotate the aircraft for fly-away, I found the stick frozen. I didn't know it at the time, but the fallen filter had wedged into and jammed the stick. The stick wouldn't move. I didn't have time to think about ejecting. With a combination of adrenalin and twenty years of weight lifting, I slammed the stick as hard as I could. The filter broke, the stick responded, and away we went.

Training.
I hear. I forget.
I see. I remember.
I do. I understand.
I feel. I react. (Huinker)

Runners run faster in a real race than they do in practice. Poker players play better against great players than they do against average players. Business competitors make us better. We have no choice — we either advance or fail. The stiffer the competition, the better we focus. Lederer: "Your best play occurs when you are in a focused and relaxed mode. To live in the moment. Being in the moment doesn't mean you don't take into account everything you have learned from the past. It is a mental mindset, which says the past and the future, maybe more importantly, the future, don't exist. If you can destroy the past and the future, all that is left is right now." It is running the marathon but not thinking about the race, only about the lines on the road. Athletes in "the zone." It is awareness of everything that surrounds you. It's looking at the big picture in detail at the same time as the world has slowed down. I think of it as a soft Zen focus, where someone is completely relaxed but aware.

Often we don't see the light until we feel the heat. Training is supposed to give us the ability to freeze-frame a fluid pressure moment and look around to see what's going on. Calm in the face of chaos. That's the theory. Read how Brian reacted the first time he was faced with combat.

The missile flame passes in front of our nose. Bones and I are now searching the starboard side of our F-14 for any incoming MIGs. I am breathing in as much oxygen as I can take. Then I see a flare shoot out and down into the clouds. Where did that flare come from? I can't see anything to the east with the day glow, but now I know there is a bad guy out there.

Then I see them. Four aircraft, dead ahead, with their tails to us. I lock a Sidewinder missile to the closest one, ready for a kill. I look down and see the range to the Hornets at two miles. I must be behind or off course. But my timing shows me right on. "Honda 51 has four aircraft on our nose for two miles. Showing them friendly?!?" What is going on? Who the hell is up here, right now, on our strike route?

1 + 1 = 2. It's gotta be them. I unlock my Sidewinder. But what are they doing out in front of me?

Doesn't matter. "Hornets passing down our left," I inform Clam.

"Visual."

I can tell by his call he doesn't know what they are doing either. We are only 15 miles from the target area. Clam is over there to my left, and I now know where my Hornet wingmen are.

The radio comes alive. "SA-6 active." The SA-6 is a Russian-built SAM system that the enemy has in their arsenal of tricks. "SAM at two o'clock," the lead Hornet calls. I start looking for the missile. I never see it.

"SAMs at ten o'clock."

"Are they tracking?" someone asks.

"Where are they?"

"Two SAMs now going over the top."

As I look up, I see them. Two plumes of smoke racing through the sky in a perfect formation. They are a good 10,000 feet above my Tomcat.

"Those SAMs no factor." We continue in to take care of the target area and then turn around. "Two SAMs at two o'clock." Bones and I are looking everywhere but don't see these new threats. I maneuver the Tomcat anyway, and then we see them.

"One's tracking on me," I hear over the radio. Pure fear. Whoever that is, his voice goes up another octave. "It's guiding on me." And then he is quiet.

Another voice comes on the radio just grunting and straining. Oh, boy, this is not going well. My brain and thinking are shrinking to an unbelievably small size. Here I am, over enemy land, missiles are in the air, and people are screaming on the radio.

After another overflight of the target, I begin our turn back to the south. Bones and I see it at the same time. Another missile is fired, and it heads our way. At our three o'clock, all I can see is the fire from its exhaust as it rides up through the clouds, but it is definitely tracking on us. Things start to go into real slow motion in our cockpit.

"Bones, I got one tracking us at three o'clock."

"Yeah, I got it too." He sounds pretty calm compared to what I feel. I roll the Tomcat on its back and pull. It is still there. Damn. I roll our Tomcat back upright while we try to outrun it, and then it goes stupid. It goes vertical and then pitches back down to earth through the clouds.

As we continue our turn, the sky is covered with a latticework of missile exhaust plumes and jet contrails. Out of the corner of my eye, I see three more SAMs from the west flying in a perfect echelon formation. Two of them continue to make a high arc in the sky, but the third breaks formation with its two brothers and levels out and starts a race across the sky. Bones and I watch that one very carefully. The other two continue their trajectory over the top and are no longer a factor. The one rogue missile then explodes about one-half mile to the right of our jet. Oh, I hope that didn't hit anyone.

Things are happening fast. I continue to climb and accelerate. I lose track of my wingman. I have no idea what is happening outside of my cockpit, and my situational awareness is at an all-time low. As far as I am concerned, it is Bones and me flying. That is enough for me to handle. I know from all the maneuvers that I am doing I am definitely the last one out.

Another SAM catches my eye on my nose as it holds steady. I think this one is tracking on me as well, and as I begin to maneuver I see it tip over from the vertical to the horizontal and start after one of the aircrafts in front of me. But it is a smaller missile by the looks of it because as quickly as it gets to altitude it runs out of poop and descends back into the clouds.

My airspeed is slowly climbing, as is my altitude. I select after-burner. I know this will highlight my position, but I also feel I need to get going even faster and higher. Another SAM launches on our left side bearing 150. It looks like a ballistic launch, so we continue. We are well below it.

I can't take it anymore. It is too quiet on the radios. "Honda 51 headed 180."

"Honda 52 headed 180."

Thank God Clam and Mondo are OK!

Brian lived up to Wooden's "controlled focus and directed energy." You define the moment, or it defines you.

> *Most people have no idea of the giant capacity we can immediately command when we focus all of our resources on mastering a single area of our lives. — Tony Robbins*

A major problem with poker students is the boredom of having to wait until the situation and cards allow them to play a hand. With boredom comes a lack of focus. It happens to everyone in business as they are climbing the corporate ladder. Seemingly meaningless reports, paperwork, and other mundane tasks induce ennui.

If the circumstances don't force you to become focused, you must create your own. Paul Wasicka, winner of the National Heads-Up Poker Championship and over $7 million in tournament winnings, uses meditation and deep breathing. Seidel forces himself to "find tells and betting patterns." Chuck used a hypnosis cue. The specific technique is not important. Having one is.

A leak in your game is some sort of repeated behavior that over time costs you resources — in poker, money lost. The greats are constantly trying to find their own leaks and plug them. This goes back to the fundamentals, where the best use every tool to analyze past plays.

What are the holes in your company? Every organization has leaks — somewhere in its pricing, product, place, promotion, people, finances, or the systems that hold it together. General Electric was the largest customer of Kanthal, a heating wire manufacturer. Naturally, Kanthal did everything it could to keep its primary customer happy, including accommodating last-minute change orders and expedited deliveries. It was losing money on its biggest customer. When it realized the leak, it sat down with GE and let the company know that it couldn't continue losing money. GE then helped by eliminating the inefficiencies (Rosenblatt).

All businesses and all people have leaks; some we can see ourselves, but most we can't. Asking others, including stakeholders, which behaviors can be improved always results in a better organization or person.

Kaizen is a Japanese word that means "small continuous daily improvements." You will wake up tomorrow, and you will be 90 years old. Time goes by in an instant.

> *Most pros are thinking about the game even when they are away from the game. They spend their waking hours thinking about the plays, ideas, things they could have done better. Trying to improve themselves even away from the table.* — Howard Lederer

It was midnight at Oceana Naval Base, and Brian had to go flying. I asked to attend the briefing. Interesting enough. After the briefing, I followed Brian and the other pilots, watched them get their flight suits on, and listened to a few of their jokes.

When helmets and flight suits were on, a non-com brought in some papers for the pilots to look over. He saw me and asked if I'd like to go out to the tarmac. "You bet!" I started walking out, and the non-com gave me some ear protectors.

Brian and I walked to his F-14. A ground crew was standing at attention next to the plane with soft yellow lights in their hands. Lots of F-14s were lined up. Brian let me pull on the wing to see how sturdy the $40 million plane was. He and his radar intercept officer (RIO), the back-seat person (Goose in *Top Gun*), walked around inspecting the plane.

Brian then climbed all over the plane. I looked around and saw the faint outlines of other pilots doing the same. Brian and his RIO got in. I was still standing within touching distance. The cockpit lowered. A man with yellow lights came over, pulled my left ear protector off, and said, "Don't move!" He put my ear protector back on. The engines started to roar. The plane slowly moved away, and within seconds Brian took off.

Watching the silhouette of his plane taking off, the fire of the burners from the two engines outlined against the midnight sky, it seemed like just yesterday he was born in Munich. The man I saw was no longer the boy I remembered.

It's so easy to wake up and find that you lost a day, a week, a lifetime. The simple concept of making *kaizen* improvements has dramatic and far-reaching rewards. Imagine how great any player in any endeavor will become if he makes just one improvement every day of his life.

> *Every day do something that moves yourself toward your most important goal.* — Brian Tracy

> *You're supposed to keep learning until you don't have any time left.*
> — Bill Clinton

The best players and leaders make sure they have made at least one improvement every day. Wasicka: "I learn from my opposition, some of the things that they are doing that work really well. I am always trying to pick up new strategies."

Dusty Schmidt, winner of over $4 million online, has played over 9 million hands (10-hour sessions, 18 tables) and says this:

> It all comes down to the preparation, the work you do, away from the tables. Every single day I write down the hardest decisions I was forced to make that day. And then do work away from the table to solve those situations and what I should do in the future. If you have 500 leaks in your game and you could fix five a day, in a hundred days you'd be playing pretty darn good poker. You'll just get washed away if you don't keep up.

If you practice *kaizen*, you'll be amazed at how your poker or business play gets better and better.

I always recommend that a student play 250,000 hands before he plays for money he really cares about. Other poker teachers scoff at this, saying that 10,000 hands is sufficient. I suggest the 250,000-hand threshold because I want my students to see the same situation against varying opponents and circumstances repeated so often it is ingrained in their memories. Of course, there's a big difference between playing 250,000 hands and learning from 250,000 hands.

Dusty played over 2 million hands before he had a good win rate. By that time, he'd been exposed to almost every possible situation and could remember what he'd done right or wrong and what a specific opponent had done. Being able to recall, in the smallest detail, what an opponent did is a weapon the greats have.

Women recall everything. Men nothing. Carol can remember the smallest slight I might have made (I say "might have" because I don't remember it) 50 years ago.

If you are working with a poker mentor, he will ask you about the smallest details of hands you have played. The more particulars you can recall, the more your mentor can help you. There are literally hundreds of memory games on the Internet. Playing these games ten minutes a day for a year will sharpen any mind.

Becoming an expert observer and being able to recall the smallest details pay dividends.

Remembering exactly what someone did during a previous negotiation will help you to make a better decision in this negotiation.

I see a young tattooed male, body piercings everywhere, with his baseball cap on backward at a poker table and make some immediate assumptions about his style of play. The information we receive interacts with values, perceptions, and our culture. We can't do anything about these psychic burdens, but we must try to recognize how they shape our lenses. A bias or assumption is often a mental shortcut we use to try to make sense of a complex circumstance, leading us in the wrong direction. Far too many critical decisions by those who thought their assumption or bias was fact, when it wasn't even close, have resulted in disaster. We'll revisit this concept in the chapter on decision making.

There's a hidden bias if you are an extrovert, and it's one I wish I'd known long ago. Although the general population is about evenly split between extroverts and introverts, over 90% of those in a leadership position are extroverts (Ones and Dilchert). Extroverts tend to have dominant personalities and want to be decision makers, but they don't listen well. That's the hidden bias — you need to listen more carefully, especially to your proactive stakeholders. It's the difference between Patton the autocratic dictator who listened to no one and Lincoln the empathetic listener.

The anchor bias. There is a psychological test showing that most people give too much weight to an initial reference point, to the information first discovered. The subject is given two cities he has never heard of and then told the distance between the cities is 1,000 miles. Later he is given two more cities he has never heard of and asked to estimate how far apart they are. The answer always centers on 1,000 miles. That's the anchor bias. His initial reference point clouds his future estimate. This next part is weird. If he is shown a nice piece of glassware and asked what he thinks it costs, his answer is close to $1,000. The anchoring effect goes beyond a simple connection.

In a cash game, I am aggressive-tight. But when I first sit down in a cash game with players I have never seen before, I will aggressively play two trash cards all the way to the river and then show my cards win or lose. I use this anchor bias, and now the table expects me to be an extreme aggressive-loose. It will pay off when I do have a strong hand.

Some people are at the other end of the spectrum: that is, they place too much weight on information recently discovered.

And there is a bias to what we think we already know. One of the regulars at my weekly riverboat game is a very tight player who plays only premium hands and never raises preflop even with AA. I know, at least I think I know, if he is in a hand and an Ace flops and he bets or just calls, the worst he has is AJ and probably something stronger. If he ever decides to bluff (I think the last time he bluffed was never) and shows his cards, I'd know I no longer know.

Which are we? Are we likely to succumb to the anchor effect, the information most recently discovered, or always think we know? None of us is baggage free. Friends and family members know our biases better than we do. Ask them. They are the best resources we can use to help us understand what we can't see in the mirror.

> *I think maintaining your composure at the poker table is one of the most important things if you want to be successful as a player. You have to realize that you can't control the luck factor, but you can control how you react to it.* — Mike Sexton

We see it all the time. A player has just been bluffed out of the winning pot or beat by what he considers to be a donkey. He's on tilt. He goes after the winning player or perhaps any other opponent with a vengeance, aggressively playing any two cards to the river. Tilt means profit to his opponents.

> *The term "full tilt" comes from medieval jousting. If a jouster rode his horse as fast as he could at his opponent, he was said to be full tilt.*

Emotion overcomes logic. Revenge play is poor play, no matter the game. I disagree with Trump's "Get mad, then get even," and prefer Powell's "Get mad, then get over it." Don't spend much time thinking about bad beats unless it's to learn something from them. Seidel: "There is no upside to thinking about stuff like that. It is wasted energy. Emotional control is critical. I have always been good at focusing on what is important and taking the emotion out of the decision. I think in terms of what's the right decision here?"

Many players who have difficulty controlling their emotions use a mindset coach, such as Sam Chauhan, CEO of Changing You. Sam doesn't know much about poker, but he helps players focus on the moment.

Deep breathing, seeing yourself in a calm environment, or just taking a break are some of the techniques we can all use to avoid tilt. If you find yourself on tilt, and can't instantly bring yourself back, walk away from the table for a few hands. In an intense negotiation, do the same when you know you have lost your cool.

When you use math such as game theory to assess your opponent's probable moves, you assume your competitor is logical. But is he? When someone is emotional, logic and predictors such as game theory become less relevant. Everyone might go on micro-tilt, ticked, but only for a minute. Leave the monkey tilt for Hellmuth. As with any critical business situation, it's important for one to step out of the minutiae of the moment and look at the big picture, the vision, the mission, the overall goal, the strategic plan. If you catch yourself overanalyzing a moment in a hand or a tournament or a negotiation, you need to break out of that funk and look at the clichéd "big picture."

> *Really good poker players play close to their vests all the time and are*
> *not really bothered when they lose . . . that's true in markets too.*
> *— Andy Redleaf*

The best players know their own tipping points. How much of a preflop bet does it take to make me fold? Will I fold to a four times the big blind bet? Five times? Postflop will I fold to a 70% pot bet, or will it take more than a pot bet? Do I mask my tipping points?

They know the point at which they are no longer willing to risk resources to gain market share or chase potential profit.

When do you cut your losses? How much time do you give to something before you call it a success or failure? How long do you compete before you give up and move on to something else? This goes back to some of the discussion in the chapter on strategic thinking and knowing your value proposition to your customers. Are you a price leader such as McDonald's or Walmart? Are you a project specialist such as Apple or Bic? If you know your customers' value proposition, it helps to decide if it's time to cut your losses on a project or product.

Sometimes, to get across the pond, you have to skate on thin ice. Poker players call this alligator blood. I don't mean no fear. Fear is useful. I'm talking about having control over your fear. In poker, we learn how to regard the chips as just chips as opposed to the amount of money in the pot and what that money means to us and our families. In business, we learn to regard our resources as a means to an end as opposed to the millions at stake.

The best way to learn how to control fear is to confront it. Avoidance breeds more avoidance and results in a downward depression. The only way out is to brave through. Face up to those snakes, that precipice. A small worm the first day, a slightly larger worm the next. Then a baby snake. A small baby step up the ladder each day.

They know the point at which they are no longer willing to risk resources to gain market share or chase potential profit.

Reagan fired the air traffic controllers. Clinton vetoed legislation he supported to send a message to the Republican Congress. Both understood the concept of standing up to the bully. Despite the command of the Secret Service and the urging of all his advisers, Bush II refused to leave the White House as Flight 93 was headed there.

When I talk about standing up to the bully, I don't mean running to the principal or your attorney. I mean taking care of it yourself.

All of our sons were small until their late teens. Chuck was the smallest in his class, and he took a beating at least once a week on the school bus. Brian was hassled daily, especially from three much bigger upperclassmen. Everyone picked on Joe. No one came running to Dad for help. They knew I would have told them to face it on their own. They did. Joe became a several-degree karate black belt. Chuck became a world-class athlete. Brian took up weight lifting and wrestling.

One day, when Carol was on her way to the high school to pick up Brian, she passed a mob of students in the park. It was obvious a fight was going on. Carol, also a black belt, considered breaking up the fight but decided she should meet Brian at the usual time. She couldn't find him, so she decided to return home.

Brian came home late with clothes torn and a battered body. One of the bullies had come at him again in the park. This time, after years of getting beat up, Brian was ready. His opponent went home with a broken arm and a few teeth missing. No one ever bothered Brian again.

Joe Cirulli writes the following.

I heard Earl Nightingale say, "Circumstance does not make the man, it reveals him to himself."

I attended Notre Dame High School in upstate New York. I participated in most sports, and wrestling was one of them. My high school was so small I had to wrestle in the 165-pound weight class even though I weighed only 145. I always believed in the saying, "It's not the size of the dog, it's the size of the fight in the dog."

One night we had to travel to another town to compete. I had been sick for a number of days before the match, and the bus ride didn't help. To top it off, my opponent was not only bigger than me, he was also tough.

The first minute of my match went fine, until suddenly I found myself on my back! For the next minute I fought getting pinned. I survived, but this was only the first of three periods. Twenty seconds into the second period I got put on my back again. For the next minute and 40 seconds I kept my opponent from holding both my shoulders down for the required one second. I made it through round two, but I was totally exhausted.

Third period. The ref yells, "Wrestle!" and within two seconds I'm on my back again. My opponent gets one of my shoulders down. I decide I've had enough and let my other shoulder go down to the mat. I see the ref's hand go up ready to signify the pin. I can't do it. I raise my other shoulder. The ref lowers his hand. My opponent goes into overdrive. I know the period has to be over soon. I can fight this a few seconds longer. I look up at the clock. It's only been 32 seconds. I decide to quit again. The ref's hand goes up, but I can't let him do it! I find the strength to raise one shoulder a fraction of an inch off the mat. I survive again knowing the round has to be over. I look at the clock. One minute left! I can't fight anymore. I'm absolutely shot. My shoulders drop down one more time. Same response. I just can't quit. I fight to the end and never get pinned.

When I walked slowly off the mat my coach and the entire team came to congratulate me. I couldn't understand it. I just had the crap beaten out of me. So why are they congratulating me?

Eventually, I understood. Winning isn't everything. Quitting is. I understood that just like winning, quitting is a habit. I realized if I had quit, I might always quit when things got tough. I look back on that event, and when things get tough today, I know I can hold on just a little bit longer.

"Circumstance does not make the man, it reveals him to himself." I think back to that match some 40 years ago and still feel proud that I didn't quit.

The strongest steel comes from the hottest fire. Everyone goes through adversity and suffering. The key is how we deal with it. One way is to stand back and realize that everyone goes through such times, that hard times are temporary. That alone gets rid of the "why me?" syndrome and often provides perspective.

Another technique is called reframing. Changing your point of view changes your viewpoint. What some view as stumbling blocks others view as stepping stones. George Arimond, business owner, consultant, and department chair: "I pursue something, and if I come up against a wall I look at it and say, 'Is there a way for me to get through that wall, go over the wall, or do an end run around the wall?'"

Ron Rubens, creator of the World Poker Tour Camp: "The smart people in life are the ones that when they hit a road block just push through it. A lot of people give up at that point, they just stop and stick where they are in life. There are a small number of people who continue to persist."

Mike Krzyzewski (Coach K): "When you are passionate, you always have your destination in sight, and you are not distracted by obstacles. Because you love what you are pursuing, things like rejection and setbacks will not hinder you in your pursuit."

Challenges make us better, give us more experience, more confidence. When we run out of every possible option, we find a new one. Darwin at his best. Great players, poker or business, don't let bad events change their hearts. Trump: "The only time you will be a failure is if you quit trying. Winners keep on going." Trump deserves respect not for all of his successful, transaction-based deals but for how he persisted when he was billions under water. Get long pink ears and a battery for a backbone.

> *Determination and stick-to-it-iveness are two qualities that you absolutely have to have. — Phil Gordon*

> *When thwarted try again; harder, smarter. Persevere relentlessly.*
> *— John Wooden*

Fraud, lying, cheating, greed, cruelty, and immorality are everywhere. My biggest disappointment in life is how much of it exists. I'm sure it's been there as long as humans have been around, but it's a far cry from the way I was brought up. It is the black sail of Achilles. It is those who would steal the Lord's Last Supper (Walters).

Poker has more than its fair share of unsavory characters, especially in the lower and middle ranks. Dusty Schmidt's understatement: "I've had some experiences I wasn't too pleased with in the poker industry." There have been scandals at Ultimate Bet and Absolute Poker similar to those at Enron and Worldcom.

There is a time to fight, but it should be your last resort. A fight is a lot easier to get into than to get out of. Ask George W. But, if you are up against evil, you have no other choice. Put your helmet on and go on the field. As will be discussed in the chapter on decision making, logic, not emotion, must dictate your engagement.

Decide up front what victory means to you. Define what a win is. Then realize it's going to be a costly use of your resources. Appreciate the psychological stress it will cause you, your family, and your people. Ensure that everyone at least understands and hopefully supports your rationale.

Poker players plan ahead and know what they will do depending on what might appear on the board, who bets and how much, and a host of other factors. They are proactive, not reactive. They know which punch they will throw depending on what the opponent does. If you are planning ahead, your opponent's punch won't be nearly as effective as your counterpunch. Until recently, all law enforcement was primarily reactive. Investigators didn't go around looking for murders, they investigated those that occurred. 9/11 changed that. The FBI is no longer reactive. Today it tries to stop attacks before they happen.

Poker is a turn-based game. Your competitor does one thing, you do another, then he does something else. Business is sometimes similar in that a company makes a move, then a competitor makes its move, and so on. In poker, we can clearly and instantly see the moves our opponents make. In business, even if we are proactive and plan what to do if our competitor does X, we don't often see the move our competitor has made until long after he made it, and by that time our counterpunch might not have the result we intend.

You might have to employ some who enjoy, and even relish, the battle. We have a female divorce attorney in town who just loves to go after husbands. She tears them apart in depositions and goes for the jugular every time. Wives in the know hire her. Every husband's attorney fears her.

One successful approach is to attack with overwhelming force, forgetting the concept of a proportional response. Focus on changing your opponent's payoffs, not by calling but by continually, aggressively raising. Never blink. Attack. Attack. Always attack. The exception, of course, is when you are trapping. That is when your hand or product is best but your competitor hasn't figured that out yet.

When someone plays high-limit or no-limit cash, the game becomes less about what someone holds and more about a combination of aggressive betting and being able to read your opponent.

Don't play in games you can't afford to play in. — Mike Sexton

If your company can't afford the loss, you shouldn't be in the chase. You'll play tight and scared. And you'll abort your mission too soon and too often. Similarly, unless you have an absolute winner, avoid the risk of putting all your company eggs into one basket.

The banking crisis is an excellent example of exorbitant risk taking. Most of that risk was taken with the unspoken understanding that the government wouldn't let the big banks fail. The government should have. The strong would have survived, and the taxpayer wouldn't have been left wondering why he was holding the bag. The dotcoms spent millions for Super Bowl ads only to see their lavish spending bring them under quickly.

Every defeat is a lesson. Wasicka: "As I was learning, I learned the most from the hands I lost, not the hands I won." When successful pros lose, they analyze hands, opponents, strategies, everything. The more they lose, the more they learn, and eventually the more they win.

The really smart ones learn from the mistakes of others, not just from their own. History often repeats itself because few listen the first time. Robert Kiyosaki, author of *Rich Dad*: "If you want to go somewhere, it is best to find someone who has already been there."

We need to take lessons from the poker greats. We won't live long enough to make every mistake, so we must study those who have been in similar situations, see what they have done right, see what they have done wrong — and avoid the wrongs. Jeff Amrein, CEO of Amber Platform Technologies and owner of Hog Wild Poker: "You learn so much more from your failures than your successes." The smart leader learns from his losses. The great leader learns from the losses of others.

You will learn more by the times you got kicked in the seat of the pants than you do from a pat on the back. — Joe Chilsen

One technique I use with new poker students is a computer opponent for them to practice against. There are several on the market, but I think the best is Poker Academy Pro (no, I didn't get something for this product endorsement). The program allows you to play against various types of computer opponents and teaches you good habits, valuable skills, and many important lessons. I prefer starting off poor college students here because I know the investment they make in the program will be far less than they will lose playing on their own. Learners can also go to any of the various online poker sites and use play money. The sites are giving away the drug to get you hooked so that eventually you start playing for real money.

You recall the story of Brian having to turn off the engine at 30,000 feet and having to land the plane without starting it up again. Lots of potential sting. No longer does the military train its pilots that way. Today it's all on simulators. Carol crashed trying to land on an aircraft carrier — on a simulator. Simulators do help the learning process, but they have no sting.

MBA students can play all kinds of business games, many of which are well thought out. Although the learning experience is useful, they sting only when you get a knock on your ego or a poor grade (but no one gets a poor grade these days).

As poker students start to play for real money, they experience a sting when they lose. Jean-Robert Bellande, with over $1 million in tournament winnings, is known for often going broke. He knows what sting is all about. Almost every multi-millionaire poker player you see on television has gone broke. Some several times.

As the first-time entrepreneur fails, he feels the sting. The sting is important. We learn from our stings. The trick is to make sure the sting isn't so big that we lose everything.

How do you know the light unless you have been in the dark? The Chinese language is composed of over 30,000 symbols. The word *disaster* has two symbols: "danger" and "opportunity" (another interpretation of these symbols is "danger" and "crucial point").

During the poker world championship, Jack "Treetop" Straus shoved all of his chips in. He lost the hand. When he looked down, he noticed he'd forgotten to bet one chip. Although down to essentially nothing, he won the tournament, giving rise to the expression "a chip and a chair."

Cirulli was homeless and went into McDonald's to buy a Diet Coke. When he went to pay, he found he had only 12¢ to his name. As he walked out, Cokeless, he looked to the sky and told God, "Thank you for this moment. I know I will never be in this position again."

That hand is over. Deal the next one.

Augie Nieto started off in business by building a computerized exercise cycle. He then put it in his van and tried to get any health club to lease or buy it. His company, Life Fitness, became the world leader in computerized fitness equipment. Augie was dealt a bad beat. A really bad beat. He contracted amyotrophic lateral sclerosis, also known as Lou Gehrig's disease. It's a disease of the nerve cells in the brain and spinal cord that control voluntary muscle movement. Nieto: "You can't control what happens to you, you can control how you respond. ALS has given me a unique perspective. I was so caught up in my ability to raise my hand and take credit for what I did. Today I get so much joy being a coach."

In many countries, people live in what we'd consider in the United States to be extreme poverty and unlivable conditions. Yet, if you visit these people in Ecuador, Peru, Mexico, Guatemala, Jamaica, and the Dominican Republic, you'll notice one thing. Despite their lack of clean water and shoes and their homes made of cardboard or scrap wood, they still know how to laugh and smile. These people know how to face what we'd consider as demoralizing and life-crippling difficulties and stay positive in the hope of a better life (Rosenblatt).

Why did Louis Zamperini survive? His B-24 was shot down over the Pacific. He and his pilot manage to get into a tiny rubber raft. For days, the sun beats down. On day 27, a Japanese plane strafes them with a machine gun, deflating the raft. The ever-present sharks sense a meal. Zamperini beats them off with an ore while trying to inflate the raft. On day 33, the pilot gives up his spirit and dies. Louis cooks meals in his mind, sings songs such as "White Christmas," eats a bird that comes too close, and learns to love the smell of his own earwax. After seven weeks, it looks like rescue, but it turns out to be Japanese sailors. He is sent to a prison camp. When the Japanese find out his celebrity (he was the youngest U.S. distance runner ever to compete in the Olympics), they target him for special torture. Yet he still thinks of a better place in his mind. Why did he survive while so many others didn't? He had a choice. He could have dwelled on his suffering and pain. He chose to think of good things. He stayed positive.

If you've seen the movie *The Pursuit of Happyness*, modeled after the life of Christopher Gardner, then you get a pretty good picture of an individual who overcame tremendous obstacles in life and business by staying positive and working hard. He overcame poverty, family struggles, life in and out of shelters with his toddler son, and other incredible challenges. Today he is the CEO of his own stockbrokerage firm, a motivational speaker, and a philanthropist (Rosenblatt).

The more difficult the journey, the more rewarding the accomplishment.

You should care but not too much. It's just chips. Won $200,000 last night. Lost $200,000 tonight.

I can't recall the name of the gentleman, but he was a negotiator between the United States and Russia back when it looked like we would blow each other off the earth. The world was literally on the brink. He told me that he approached every session with the attitude of "care but not too much." He said that, if he cared too much, it was difficult to stay calm, to control himself; rational thought was impossible, and it became too easy to do things he knew he shouldn't. The world didn't blow up, so he must have known what he was doing. Caring too much makes you emotional and impedes your logic. It takes away clarity.

All great poker and business players have outside distractions, giving them some sort of balance. Negreanu plays golf with Ivey and other poker buddies, sometimes for $10,000 a hole.

Chuck writes the following.

The next tournament was in San Salvador. My roommate and I were in our hotel room watching CNN. Suddenly, there was a loud blast, and the lights and TV went black. We went out on the porch to see what had happened and spotted a fire in the hills about half a mile away. The rebels had bombed a generator.

Within the next 15 minutes, two more bombs went off. All the players staying at the hotel were running from balcony to balcony, trying to get a better view of the proceedings. There was sporadic red tracer fire within blocks of our hotel, and helicopters were moving in, firing on the rebels below. It was sort of like watching a *Rambo* film without the popcorn.

Suddenly, we saw more tracer bullets, and a stray bullet whistled through the trees in front of our balcony, causing everyone to jump. The next few hours were a mix of explosions, gunfire, and sirens. Occasionally, I could hear screams and orders being yelled out.

It was starting to get late, and I had a match the next day. I decided to try to get some sleep. Since the air conditioning was broken, I left the door to my balcony open and drifted off to sleep to the sound of sporadic gunfire.

In tournament play, rule number one is to protect your stack, especially against superior opponents. A key to protecting your stack is to keep the pot small by playing passively. This means careful play in marginal situations. Depending on the skill of your opponent and the situation, you will often avoid playing a big pot with second high pair. When out of position, check the flop and then fold or call. When in position, either call or bet enough to get your opponent to do what you want.

From an interview with Phil Gordon:

Student: "Do you have a favorite hand you like to play?"
Phil: "Any hand I'm playing against Charley."

I am a good player. Phil is a great player. We both know who is better. When you know your skill is superior to that of a competitor, you have the odds on your side. When you know he is superior, avoid the confrontation.

Superior players often avoid playing hands against another superior player. Negreanu would be very cautious against Brunson. Against me, Phil wouldn't even look at his cards. Google should be careful going up against Microsoft. But Google wouldn't be cautious against a startup since its experience and resources will help it to win almost every battle.

Taking the long view in business, we need to stay in business. Revenues must exceed expenses. Consider the new fast-food burger franchise in a market already covered by several McDonald's franchises. It wouldn't want to play a big pot against a more experienced and skilled foe; more appropriate would be a strategy of slow growth and picking its spot.

The entrepreneur or business leader first needs to think about the niche he wants to fill when considering a market dominated by a larger, more well-known opponent. This is the small stack going up against not only the big stack but also the big stack that has more skill. As serendipitous as it sounds, what often happens in these situations is that the entrepreneur will try a few things, find out if he can fill a niche, and see what happens.

Your table image is how your opponents view you. It is your brand at the table. Your true identity might be different, but perception is reality. It is how others view you. My son Brian's brand is immediately established by taking his plane to the edge of, and sometimes slightly beyond, the envelope. I already mentioned the brands of Negreanu, Jordan, and Oprah. Think of Milken, Lay, and Madoff.

A company often selects its brand after it has developed the product but before it enters the market. In poker, you design your table image around your comfort zone. Barry Greenstein is viewed as one of the tightest players and selectively uses that image to his advantage (Huinker).

In tournament play, it's relatively easy to change your table image from table to table. On the flip side, if you have invested a lot of time at a particular table establishing an image, it's lost when you move to another table. In business, it's very difficult to change your brand image. Honda had a great deal of difficulty gaining market share when it first entered the U.S. car market after being known as a small engine manufacturer for so long (Huinker).

Via television, some poker players have been able to create their own brands. In addition to Negreanu, we have Brunson, Ivey, Hellmuth, Duke, and Dwan.

As Mike Sexton was relating a story about Chip Reese, he said that a big difference between great players and good players is that the greats can play their A game all the time. Tilt isn't part of their game. When they are tired, they don't play. In one word, *discipline*. Once my students have progressed beyond the basics, this is the mantra they must repeat when they look at their cards: "I am playing my A game, all the time, relentlessly, tirelessly."

No different in business. Especially if we are tired or content. Look at how Apple rose from the dead as competitors such as Dell became complacent.

Poker will humble you. Business will humble you. Battle will humble you. Life will humble you. Experience is expensive. It's the comb nature gives us when we are bald.

> *Virtually all of the greats have gone broke at least once in their careers, and I'm no different. The key is to learn something from the experience.*
> — *Daniel Negreanu*

Almost every great leader has first been a great failure. Edison: "I have not failed, I have found 10,000 ways that don't work." He regarded every failure as a step toward success. Disney went bankrupt before he made it. He didn't give up. He learned what not to do.

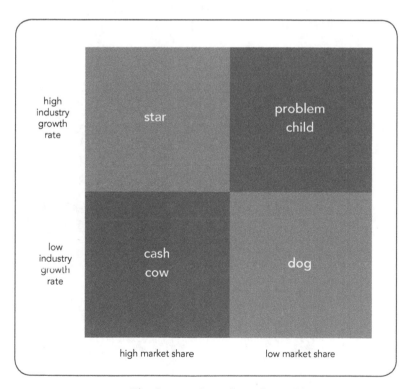

Figure 3.4 The Boston Consulting Group Matrix

Knowing your product is part of knowing your business self. The Boston Consulting Group Matrix is a traditional way to look at products (Figure 3.4). Once you know where your products fall, you can figure out what to do with them.

The horizontal axis represents the company's market share. The vertical axis, depending on which version is used, represents either the company's growth rate or the industry's growth rate. I prefer to use the industry's growth rate since it will lead to the discovery of the best opportunities. If you aren't familiar with this model, a quick synopsis is to shoot the dogs, maintain your cash cows to provide funding to protect your stars, and move your problem children to stars.

In poker, I always try to place each opponent in my PATL (pronounced "paddle") matrix (Figure 3.5). The P stands for passive (doesn't raise much), the A for aggressive (raises a lot), the T for tight (plays few hands), and the L for loose (plays lots of hands).

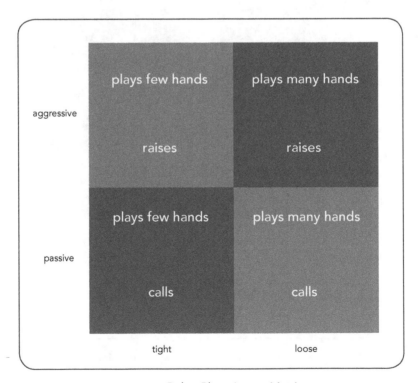

Figure 3.5 Poker Player's PATL Matrix

As a student is learning to play poker, I keep him in the aggressive-tight quadrant. I want this to be his initial comfort zone. More specifically, be very selective about the hands played, but be very aggressive (raise a lot) with those hands. Notice how this corresponds to the star quadrant of the Boston Consulting Group Matrix. The best use of limited business resources (money, time, and talent) is to concentrate on those products for which the industry's growth rate is positive and that have a solid market share (premium hands).

LG is noted for its aggressive-tight play by entering markets that it is certain are profitable as long as it introduces superior products (Leahy). The newbie in business should focus on being aggressive-tight with his products, but as he gains experience he should move toward being aggressive-loose (Figure 3.6). Apple's play is aggressive-loose as the company takes several innovative ideas and markets them before any other company (Leahy).

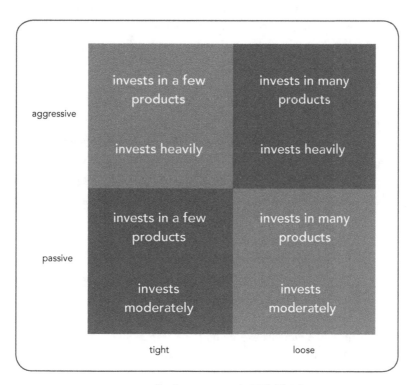

Figure 3.6 Businessperson's PATL Matrix

As the student progresses in poker, in terms of both skill and bankroll, I begin to increase his range of hands. His comfort zone increases as he learns he can and should selectively adopt the style of an aggressive-loose player: that is, at times play many hands and raise with them. Again, see how that corresponds to the problem-child portion of the Boston Consulting Group Matrix. Once we have sufficient resources, we can look at our problem children. If we have a product with a low market share and the industry growth rate is high, what do we have to do to take that product from a problem child to a star?

As an aside, keeping a star in the star quadrant is difficult and requires many resources. Good competitors will try to figure out how they can take their problem children to stars by increasing their market share and dislodging your position. As military and business leaders understand, it often costs more to hold onto an objective than it took to reach it.

Winners enjoy themselves. They don't play poker just because they make money, they simply love the game. Business leaders love their game too. I had a student who was fortunate to have several good-at's and love-to's, providing him with three possible careers. When I asked him which would be the most fun, he immediately knew his future.

Can you laugh every day?

Jerry Noyce, in addition to being a CEO, is a Tennis Hall of Famer. Over 30 years ago, I was running a tennis tournament. One of the rules I had posted was that a player would be penalized one game for each five minutes he was late for his match. Jerry and his doubles partner went to lunch with their opponents. When they all arrived a few minutes late, I told them they were all penalized one game and the score was 2-2. Jerry turned to the others and said, "At least we all held serve."

When Brian was twelve, his appendix burst. As he was about to be operated on, he asked the doctor, "Will I be able to play the piano after this operation?" The doctor replied, "Of course." Brian shot back, "That's great, because I can't play it now."

As we ran to the departing Venice train, I said to Carol, "If you had been ready on time, we would have caught the train." She said, "If you hadn't rushed me so much, we wouldn't have to wait so long for the next one."

Your Social Self

Stammtisch is German. It means you have a large table reserved for you each week at a certain time, usually at a restaurant. It's where you and your friends meet every week to discuss your lives.

It's invaluable to be able to talk about your compass, vision, mission, and situations and decisions you are facing with others you know and trust and to do so on a regular basis. The best poker players are constantly trying to learn from their fellow experts, discussing how a hand could have been played better, how they could have won more or lost less, or what they could have done differently to achieve a better outcome. They surround themselves with the most talented players. Wasicka: "It is important for me to have a core group of friends, a strong support group. I find multiple perspectives helpful." Today we can supplement these face-to-face friends with online forums.

Invite global thinkers and elder sages to your *stammtisch* even though they know nothing about your industry. These graybeards have been through a lot and have wisdom to share. Often you'll find they have gone through similar situations and can help you to apply those circumstances to your opportunities.

Almost every business belongs to an association, and within that association roundtables are common. Within an industry, they allow you to meet with those who are facing, or will face, the same problems you are. During your sessions, everyone must give as well as take. In addition to discussing problems, each person should present something no one else knows or something he does in his organization that he thinks is the best practice in the world.

Gerry Faust created executive roundtables in the health club industry, with each having 12–15 club owners and general managers who meet three times a year for up to two days. "The key to the roundtable is learning," he explains. "In a typical meeting experience, members will identify important issues, explain them, clarify for the group, and then jointly brainstorm and suggest alternative solutions. At other times, a major topic will be jointly requested and discussed — often from many different viewpoints — with several members offering new ideas, alternative ways of looking at things, or simply a new way of dealing with an age-old problem."

> *Obama seems to have understood that, as a networking tool, poker is the most efficient pastime of all. Instead of walking down fairways forty yards apart from each other, throwing elbows in the paint, or quietly hunting pheasant or muskie, poker buddies are elbow to elbow all night, competing and drinking and talking. The experience can tell them a lot about the other fellow's ability to make sound decisions, whether parliamentary or electoral, tactical or strategic. — James McManus*

Regular poker games are a *stammtisch*. Harding, FDR (the New Deal and the Square Deal both came from poker), LBJ, Truman, Eisenhower, Nixon — all played with other politicians, as much to learn what everyone was thinking as for the camaraderie.

> *Most professionals do lead balanced lives with a wide circle of friends.*
> *— Johnny Chan*

Jerry Noyce and Lyle Berman went to the University of Minnesota. Lyle doesn't remember Jerry, but Jerry remembers that Lyle would come over every week, spend a few hours playing poker with Jerry's roommates, take all of their money, and leave. Andy Redleaf took tennis lessons from Jerry when Andy was fourteen. When Jerry needed some serious money for acquisitions, Andy helped him. Chilsen: "It's not about keeping score, but it's about doing things for other people. In turn, people will help you naturally."

All of us have goals. And whether we realize it or not, we determine which goals are more important. Once our priorities are set, we automatically spend most of our time and effort on our top goal, some on our second goal, less on our third goal, and so on. The key to balance is keeping family among your top goals.

Your Physical Self

For his 90th birthday, his friends decided to surprise Harold with a hooker. When the sensuous 21 year old arrived at his door, he asked, "What are you doing here?" "I'm here to give you super sex," she replied. He thought for a moment and said, "I'll take the soup."

The players with the most stamina and focus usually win. — Tony Hsieh

In some tournaments, you can easily play for 14 hours straight and come back the next day and play for another 14 hours. You can see why the center of tournament gravity has shifted to the younger players, especially those who have the endurance to last.

This goes back partially to your compass. Those who live true to their inner cores, combining their talents and what they love to do, have contentment that translates into both longer life and extended cognitive function.

Have you ever noticed how fast some presidents age while others age normally? Hard jobs can take their toll. Both Bushes exercised daily. How many top executives do you see out of shape? If you don't use a part of your body, it won't work well when you need it.

Make a decision you are going to live to be 80 years old, or more, and begin today to do whatever you have to do to achieve that goal. Take excellent care of your physical health. You need high levels of energy to bounce back from discouragement. — Brian Tracy

A few decades after this book is published, readers will have nanobots implanted in their bodies, killing cancer, keeping them healthy, perfectly toning muscles. Until that happens, you need to treat your body as if it's the only one you will ever have. Live true to your compass, exercise, and eat right.

Rest is essential to your health. When the Lord said to rest on the Sabbath, he knew what he was talking about. Poker is rest for those who don't play professionally. Even in Obama's pre-POTUS days, "It was boys' night out — a release from our legislative responsibilities" (Link). It was "a fun way for people to relax and share stories and give each other a hard time over other senators — including Republicans" (Obama).

> To always play your A game, you must be physically and mentally ready. — Paul Wasicka

Anyone who thinks the nickel-ante poker and related shenanigans were merely good fun should consider their underlying purpose — to help the crippled FDR decompress with friends every night after dealing with the Depression and, in his third and fourth terms, the most devastating war the world has ever known (McManus).

Without rest, we cannot reflect. Without reflection, we cannot learn from the past. If we don't learn from the past, we will make poor decisions.

The more specialized and myopic we become, the more our minds contract to fit within the boxes of our fields. We become more interdependent and less independent. The more we exercise and expand our minds beyond our boxes, the more regularly we are put in positions in which we must make difficult decisions, the better we become at recognizing the key elements of psychology and numbers and the relationships between them. The result is a natural ability to play our best and make solid decisions.

In class, I act as a coach. For those who are interested in poker, I also coach them after class at least once a week. A few years ago I created two separate training programs. Each is a year long. One is intended to produce a great decision maker, the other a great poker player. Most who say they want to be great wash out before we get going when I outline the next year of their lives. It's far more intense and demanding than anything I do in my university classes or after class. It's not putting a toe in the water, it's being held under water. It is comparable to a year of military basic, combat training, and POW camp. I am less of a coach and more of a dictator. I demand their lives for 52 weeks of learning, practicing, and executing everything in this book and much more. It is intense physical, mental, spiritual, and social training designed to make one the master of all. I'm not trying to kill them, just trying to make them the best they can be. I push to the limit Wooden's dictum that "Success is a peace of mind which is a direct result of self-satisfaction in knowing you made the effort to become the

Know yourself first. — Socrates

best of which you are capable." They must sign a contract for a strict code of behavior, including random drug tests, no alcohol, and a host of other requirements. I haven't had anyone finish either program.

Know Your Competitors

If you know the enemy and know yourself,

you need not fear the result of a hundred battles. — Sun Tzu

Before Sherman went against Hood in the battle at Atlanta, he interviewed every person who had known him at West Point. Understanding Hood's personality gave Sherman the clues to understand how Hood would defend. Sherman crushed Hood.

Watch your opponents and perceive how they play the game.

Any background that you can pick up about your opponents is only

going to help you at the table. — Mike Sexton

One reason Charlie Nesson uses poker in his Harvard law classes is to get his students to see things from the opponent's point of view. If you know your opponent, can get into his skin, understand his spiritual, mental, social, and physical makeup, you'll understand his viewpoint. One's natural self dominates over time. You will know who is smarter, more experienced. Every question you answered about yourself in the previous section you must try to answer about your competitors.

Bill Russell: "I blocked most shots before most opponents ever started to take their shot." It's the same in any game where you have to think several steps ahead. In poker, it's the meta-game. What do I hold? What do I think my opponent holds? What does my opponent think I hold? And so on.

> *Let the table dictate how you are going to play. Your play is a response to what they are doing. You really tailor your game to whatever table you are at and the changing conditions. — Eric Seidel*

When Lederer talks about something called "the second guess," he is referring to two things. First, he doesn't know what his opponent has; second, he doesn't know how his opponent will play it. But there are some indications of how he will play it.

There are four ways to predict your competitor's moves. First, and this isn't politically correct, you must profile. In poker, I use specific observable characteristics (body, dress, accessories, verbal language, interaction with others) and background information (via friendly conversation) to profile opponents in the PATL matrix (see Figure 3.5, page 98). For example, if I find out a player drives a Harley, wears a large watch, has a pile of ante chips, and pulls out a money clip with lots of Benjamins, I tentatively conclude he is aggressive. If I see someone with chips stacked precisely, wearing a conservative shirt and pants and shined shoes, who pulls out a wallet with everything perfectly in place, I put him in the tight category. Although profiling provides some clues and is useful, it's the least effective of the four methods.

Second, understand what your opponent is saying. In poker, this is body language, tells. Understanding body language is highly effective in face-to-face business negotiations too.

The average player looks at only a few pieces of information when trying to read an opponent. The best players look at the whole picture. Chris Ferguson, who holds a PhD in computer science and is a winner of many World Series of Poker events, takes eight seconds before he makes his play. In addition to disguising clues to the strength or weakness of his hand, it gives him time to think about the whole situation.

In poker parlance, these are tells or body language, physical signs that an opponent is comfortable or uncomfortable with his hand or the situation. Professional players know not only how to read these signs but also how to hide their own or give off false tells.

These physical clues are directly transferable in face-to-face negotiations and even easier to use in a business setting because the other side is seldom schooled in awareness of the information it is giving away. Talk at the poker table is the same as labor and management, especially when it occurs at big points in a game.

Third, keep track of moves made so far in the game. A good predictor of future behavior is past behavior during the game. Does he always raise with 99 or just call and see the flop? Patton could foresee Rommel's likely moves. Even though dyslexic, he'd read Rommel's book and could predict his moves.

Chad Brown, with several final table finishes and over $3 million in tournament winnings: "When I'm sitting at the table even for 30 minutes with people I don't know, I can tell a lot about them. Poker is about incomplete information, so you can take that incomplete information, and you have to make an analysis of how you want to play against each of those players" (McManus).

Fourth, and by far the most important, is past behavior in life. A major influence on behavior is parents. In past generations, religion had a major impact, but that is less so today. Behavior is also influenced by things that usually change over time, such as friends, co-workers, attitudes, learning, and culture (Lewin). So the more we know about the influences on one's conduct, the easier it is to predict future actions. Most importantly, the best predictor of future behavior is past behavior, especially what your opponent has done under extreme pressure. Is his pattern always attack or "two steps forward, one step back"? In the stock market, traders call it "the trend is your friend," and it applies directly to understanding competitors. With few exceptions, that jerk in third grade is still a jerk when he's 80, and the person who was nice in third grade is still nice at 80. Does anyone really think Lucy is going to let Charlie Brown kick the football?

Wasicka and other top poker professionals use YouTube and other televised recordings to learn what their opponents have done in the past.

A firm that understands its competitor's behavior has a much higher chance of succeeding than one that doesn't. When competitors collaborate and form partnerships, they have the chance to learn about each other's behavior at a much deeper level. "Competitive collaboration also provides a way of getting close enough to rivals to predict how they will behave when the alliance unravels or runs its course" (Hamel, Doz, and Prahalad). For example, the firm can understand how a competitor responds to price changes and how it prepares to launch new products. This knowledge can give the firm a greater chance of success in future head-to-head battles after the partnership has ended (Fritz).

Arimond: "You need to see where they are at emotionally." If you don't know a competitor's hot buttons and how he will react when you hit one of the buttons, his response will probably be dramatically different from the one you predicted.

Figure 3.7 illustrates the relative importance of each method.

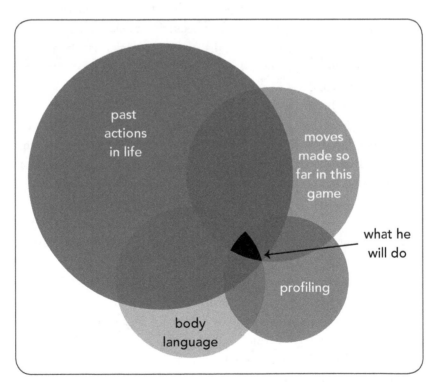

Figure 3.7 Predicting a Competitor's Moves

No man crosses the same river twice. Both the man and the river change. Bad players in poker and business who survive don't remain bad forever. They learn, and you must learn what they have learned.

Today we have Poker Tracker, Poker Stove, YouTube, and a host of other tools at our disposal. As we play online, we can type in notes about a particular player. There is a tremendous amount of information available about any competitor via engines such as Facebook, Google, and LinkedIn.

> *The great players have a sixth sense. They are able to put their opponents on a hand better than the good players. — Mike Sexton*

Howard Lederer was kind enough to review my thoughts for this section. "All of this has to become second nature," he says. "I do all of this, but I don't even think about it." The quotations below are also from him.

If you aren't a poker player, just skim this section. The point is that the best players in the world use every possible piece of information to deduce an opponent's hand.

1. Pre-game information
    The rules
        Game structure
            Cash
            Limit
                    High, Low
            No limit
            Tournament
                    Blinds go up fast
                    Blinds go up slow
    Size of initial chip stack relative to blinds and antes
    Amount of entry fee
    Number of opponents in the tournament
    Number of opponents at each table
    Hand histories of opponents
    Payout structure
        Flat
        Skewed to the top

2. Pre-hand information

    Stage of tournament

        Early

        Middle

        Bubble

        Late

    Stack (opponents', bettor's, and his)

        Short

        Medium

        Deep

        Relative to blinds and antes

    Seat relative to passives and aggressives

    Previous showdowns

    Where each opponent falls in the PATL matrix

    Next blind increase

        When

        Amount

    Number of opponents left in the tournament

    Stack size relative to those remaining in the tournament

    Number of opponents to be dealt cards

    Where the table fits in the PATL

    Opponents' skill level

        Defends blinds

        Three bets late position raisers

        Frequency of continuation bets

            Amount of continuation bet

    Opponents' non-PATL strengths and weaknesses

    What entry fee means to opponents

    What prize money means to opponents

    What are the ranges of each opponents' preflop hands?

    Position

3. Hand information

    "Top players work backwards using each betting round to eliminate certain hands."

What kind of hand does each opponent think he has?

> The best
>
> Drawing to the best
>
> Marginal
>
> Not the best and not drawing to the best

Pot size

Other opponents' betting

Number of opponents in the hand or left to act

Board texture

"It will be the actions each player takes on each successive betting round that will narrow his possible holdings."

The action taken during each round of betting

> Fold
>
> Check
>
> Check call
>
> Call
>
> Bet
>
> Raise
>
> Reraise
>
> Check raise

The force of each action

> Preflop — multiple of the big blind
>
> Postflop — percentage of the pot

Position

Who is left to act?

Probability of getting paid off

Remaining chip stack of opponent

Own remaining chip stack

"Often I am left with a single hand that can account for all of my opponent's actions."

Sexton: "Know what your image is." How does your opponent view you in the PATL? What is his perception of your brand?

When a great player finds a leak in an opponent's game, he exploits it. Does your competitor always stick with a losing product too long? Does he always neglect putting together the correct logistical systems? What does he do consistently that costs his company and gives you an advantage?

The best players know their opponents' preflop tipping points. How much of a bet does it take to get him to fold? Can I get him to fold by betting three times the big blind? Does it take four times the big blind? Five times?

Wasicka lamented that, when he was playing Chris Ferguson in a heads-up tournament, no matter how much he increased his preflop bet, Chris wouldn't fold. Ferguson is motivated by a challenge. For instance, he challenged himself to turn $0 into $10,000 with online poker. He did it. And kept going until he'd turned that $0 into over $100,000.

The best players also know their opponents' tipping points postflop. Will it be 50% of the pot? 75%? A full-pot bet? Here's the trick. The bet size is enough to define an opponent's hand and to do what we want an opponent to do.

It's invaluable finding out your competitor's psychological and financial tipping points. Beware of projecting yourself onto an opponent. We all think others think the way we do. Not true. Get into the skin of your competitor.

If you make a heavy investment at the start, will a competitor pull out of the market? How much will it take to get him to fold immediately? How about once both of you are in the race? How much will it take to get him out of the market?

With a new product, there is a market share tipping point. It's reached when you have captured the innovators and early adopters and start to penetrate the early majority. Once you have reached this tipping point, roughly a 17% market share, you are well on your way to general market acceptance.

It's always good to find a young college player at a table with stakes above what he can afford to lose. When in a hand, unless he has a monster, he is thinking about how much the money means to him. He is afraid of what he might lose as opposed to playing the hand correctly. Anytime this happens, the best players will sense a tipping point and raise him out of the hand.

Reading the table is more complicated than reading an opponent. Every table has its own personality. By far the best way to understand a table's personality (i.e., where it fits on the PATL matrix) is to watch the

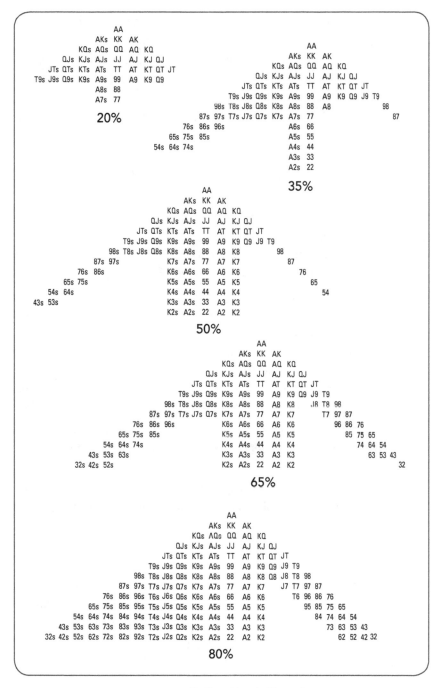

Figure 3.8 Preflop Hands Played

table for about 30 minutes before you play. If you can't watch the table, the second best way is just to play aggressive-tight at the start and watch what happens. Although certainly not exact, just by counting what percentage of preflop hands each opponent plays, you'll be able to define his likely range of hands (Figure 3.8).

Every now and then you'll consider entering with a diversified product: that is, a new product in a market you know nothing about. Before entry, investigate the competitors. Berman had no experience in the restaurant business. Steven Schussler kept politely pestering Lyle about his restaurant concept. Schussler even converted his house into his vision, including several live animals and birds. After several visits, Lyle finally became a major investor in the Rainforest Café.

Better to learn what your competitors are doing first before making the decision to get in. If that's not possible, play aggressive-tight until you know how they play.

Whether or not your opponents put you in the PATL model, they will perceive you as passive or aggressive, tight or loose. Even if you are naturally aggressive-loose, you might not have played a hand for over an hour because you went card dead. Help the perception along with comments such as "I haven't had a top-10 hand all day." If you are perceived as passive and tight, you can pull off a bluff. If you are perceived as aggressive and loose, you can make strong bets with your good hands and get paid off. Know what your competitor thinks about you, help the perception along, and use it to your advantage.

A brand of trust, quality, and caring can't help paying off in a deal. Cirulli, Krzyzewski, and Holtz are all leaders who generate trust, which helps to seal deal after deal.

Recall the basic marketing model in Figure 1.4 (page 19), which shows the various things we use to satisfy our customers, such as price, product, place, promotion, and people (our staff), and that we always know the strengths and weaknesses of each. If we know the strengths and weaknesses of our competitors' prices, products, places, promotions, and people, then we know where to attack (our strengths against their weaknesses) and where to defend (our weaknesses against their strengths).

When I first arrived for my consulting job, I told the CEO I'd like to visit all of his competitors within an eight-minute driving radius. He said he'd never been to any of his competitors and never would. We finally went. It was an eye opener for him.

Do your best to know your competitor as well as you know yourself. We have already discussed how important nature is in shaping who we are. This next step may seem extreme; not only answer every question posed about your competitor, but also dig into the background of his biological parents. The apple and the tree — the more you know about your opponent and his parents, the more predictions you can make.

Know Your Stakeholders

> *If you help enough people get what they want out of life,*
> *you'll get everything you want out of life. — Napoleon Hill*

Stakeholders are those who have an interest in or will be directly affected by your vision, mission, or something you might do. Although it's impossible to know everything about them, at a minimum have an understanding of how you can help them and how they feel.

Here are some potential stakeholders.

- Family
- Customers
- Employees and their families
- Stockholders
- Board of directors
- Boss
- Lenders
- Vendors
- Community
- Government

A common mistake among those who work in sport is spending a disproportional amount of time on the "x's and o's" as opposed to time spent learning about people. — Mike Krzyzewski

- Environmental
- Social
- Political
- Religious
- Competitors, if not adversarial

> *The most successful people in the business world, what they do best is understand people. And that's what poker is all about — people.*
> *— Tom McEvoy*

Poker is one of the few businesses in the world where you don't have any customers or employees, so other than your *stammtisch*, and most importantly your family, you have limited need for stakeholder collaboration or consideration.

Employees are one of Starbucks' primary stakeholders, but rather than calling them "employees," "staff," or even the overused "team members" they are called "partners" and treated as such. "Together we embrace diversity to create a place where each of us can be ourselves. We always treat each other with respect and dignity. And we hold each other to that standard." Your staff are entirely a reflection of you. Take special note of how Starbucks wants its customers to feel: "When our customers feel this sense of belonging, our stores become a haven, a break from worries outside, a place where you can meet with friends. It's about enjoyment at the speed of life — sometimes slow and savored, sometimes faster. Always full of humanity" (Curtis).

Harley Davidson wants its customers to be part of the club: "We ride with our customers and apply this deep connection in every market we serve to create superior value for all of our stakeholders" (Curtis).

Leaders select people with all kinds of personalities who can work together to reach a common vision. In business, if you accept the premise that you aren't really in charge, being able to understand all stakeholder personalities, including your own, becomes paramount. Arimond: "Get to know people's personalities, and try to understand what people might say or do."

There are several tools available to understand others, but the one I have found to be the most effective is the Myers Briggs Personality Profile. In short, it works by asking several questions and then placing you somewhere in the profile on the next page (Figure 3.9).

introverted sensing with thinking	introverted sensing with feeling	introverted intuition with feeling	introverted intuition with thinking
introverted thinking with sensing	introverted feeling with sensing	introverted feeling with intuition	introverted thinking with intuition
extroverted sensing with thinking	extroverted sensing with feeling	extroverted intuition with feeling	extroverted intuition with thinking
extroverted thinking with sensing	extroverted feeling with sensing	extroverted feeling with intuition	extroverted thinking with intuition

Figure 3.9 Myers Briggs Personality Profile

We won't go through each of the boxes above, but when you take the Myers Briggs you find that it pegs your dominant personality with considerable accuracy. The real benefit is how it teaches you to spot, understand, and adapt to different stakeholder personalities. Once you accept the context of another's profile when it differs from yours, you can merge your non-dominant personalities with his to help him achieve his innermost wants and desires. The result is best for all.

Since family is a primary shaper of one's personality, unless inappropriate, study an individual stakeholder's parents, spouse, and children. The other prime shaper is culture. Get to know his religion and community traditions. Family and culture provide deep clues about anyone.

Nesson uses this riddle in his law classes.

There is a queen who lives in a kingdom. She wants her son to marry the most intelligent and perceptive woman in the kingdom. To narrow the field, she gave all of the eligible maidens in the kingdom a test of intelligence and perception. Out of all the eligible women in the kingdom, three scored perfectly on the test, Ashley, Becky, and Sarah. To decide among the three, the queen devised a game.

She had them sit down and blindfolded them. She then explained that she was going to put either a red hat or a white hat on each one. They were then instructed, without looking at their own hat, to raise their hand if they saw one or two red hats on the other women. The first to tell the color of her own hat would be the winner.

The queen then placed a red hat on each of them and removed the blindfolds. Each of the women raised her hand since she saw two red hats. Some time went by. Finally, Becky said, "I have a red hat on." How did she know?

First she considered that she might have a white hat on. She then looked at it through Ashley's eyes (some might have to read the next few sentences more than once). Ashley would see the white hat on Becky and see Sarah's hand raised, which would mean that Sarah saw a red hat. Ashley would easily conclude she had a red hat on because Sarah saw a red hat and Ashley saw the white hat on Becky. Sarah could have reached the same conclusion if Becky had a white hat on.

But they sat there looking at each other with their hands up. Becky then eliminated the possibility of her hat being white because neither Ashley nor Sarah solved the puzzle. If Becky didn't have a white hat on, she concluded her hat must be red.

So what does Nesson's riddle teach us? Two things. First, we must learn to look at things as though we are our competitors and stakeholders. Second, we have to be aware of what's going on around us.

We have our own tipping points, our competitors have theirs, and so do our stakeholders.

Ticket brokers often start off with a high price to see how much tickets are worth to potential customers. If sales are few or non-existent, the price is gradually lowered until buyers are found (Giuffre).

In limit cash games, a tipping point is reached when the player can attain a long-term win rate of two big bets an hour. At a $10/$20 game, a win rate of two big bets would be $40 an hour. Once a player has reached this tipping point, he is ready for higher-stakes games.

Doug Schukar, CEO of USA Mortgage, through acquisitions and aggressive sales efforts, increased the number of loans from about $100 million to well over a billion in one year. But he forgot to include his middle managers in his plan. Almost all of them quit because of the over tenfold increase in workload. Today he looks at things through the eyes of his middle managers and includes them in planning (Macht).

Sometimes we need to think beyond our stakeholders and see if there are negative externalities. If we produce a product that harms the air, though we might not impact our usual list of stakeholders, those who live downwind might be affected, sometimes dramatically. In economics, we call this a negative externality. What we call it isn't important, but taking into account the impact of our decision is.

It's not uncommon for the vast majority of CEOs to believe they offer superior customer service. But when their customers are asked, fewer than 10% agree. Likewise, many players who don't keep a log overestimate their wins and underestimate their losses. Eventually, when their wallets are on empty, they figure it out.

At the end of my college sophomore year, I announced to my parents that I was going to hitchhike around the United States. I'm sure they didn't believe me. I left home in early June with less than $10 in my pocket and a suitcase (this was long before backpacks) with "California Please" taped on the side. My note to my parents was short: "Gone hitchhiking — be back in a few months, Love son." They knew which son it was and that I didn't have any money.

As I made my way across the United States, the little money I made I spent making sure I had a haircut and clean clothes. I seldom had to wait more than ten minutes for a ride. I sent my parents a postcard (no Internet) at least twice a week. I always managed to get a meal and a place to stay by walking up and saying, "I don't have any money. If you will give me a meal, I'll spend two hours doing any job you want." I used the same approach in finding a place to stay. No problems — ever.

As I was working my way through California, I stopped in San Diego and liked it. So I stayed for a few weeks. I got a job as an ice cream truck driver. At the end of my first two weeks, I got my first paycheck — $102. I picked up a newspaper and saw the ad "$99 air fare to Hawaii one way. Plane leaves at midnight tonight." Naturally, I was on that plane, with three dollars left over.

On the flight, I met a young Japanese woman, my age, on her way to Tokyo. I had a few leftover postcards from California, and she had cards she'd brought from Japan. We traded. I wrote on one of her Japanese postcards my parents' address and a profound message: "Great country, but I can't speak the language." I then asked her to mail it when she got to Japan.

As soon as I landed in Hawaii, I sent my parents a card. I'm sure it must have been a shock. A few days later they received the card from Japan. Looking back on my two most important stakeholders in my life at the time, I now understand how worried they must have been.

Carol is deeply religious. You'd think I would have learned what I did to my parents and should know my most important stakeholder better. We decided to go to a different Catholic church. Carol and I smiled at each other when the priest, who didn't look to be fourteen years old, walked out. I couldn't resist whispering in her ear, "He looks so young, I bet the altar boys molest him." She didn't speak to me for a month.

I encourage my students to take the golden rule platinum. It says, as opposed to treating others the way we want to be treated, we attempt to understand how the other person wants to be treated, and that's how we treat him. That's not just looking at things through another's eyes but also acting on what we see.

Know the Uncontrollables

Most opportunities and threats come from things you can't control, the things you looked at in your crystal ball, such as the following.

- Competition
- Technology
- Laws

- Changing consumer tastes
- Weather
- Demographics
- Taxes
- Culture
- Customs
- Politics
- Government
- Economy

Figure 3.10 takes the traditional marketing model and includes the concept of uncontrollables.

Figure 3.10 Uncontrollables in Marketing

A friend of mine owned a gas station on the busiest corner in the city. Three streets intersected at one spot. Stop signs on each street. Easy access to his gas station from any direction. He averaged over 600 customers a week. Very profitable. The dreaded "I'm from the government and am here to help you" arrived. The state decided this corner was way too busy, one of the roads needed to be eliminated, traffic signals and medians needed to be installed. The result: only one lane of traffic coming from one direction could get to the station; customers dwindled to 60 a week; bankruptcy ensued.

Worth repeating here is that almost every business belongs to an association. Demand that your association find the best futuristic thinkers in the world, and at every convention have them present to you which conditions they think are coming with regard to each of the uncontrollables. Listening to "future experts" is a great way to gather information, but always realize they might be trying to sell you something or be employed by the field they are representing.

Analyzing opportunities and threats is difficult since there are way too much data available. No one can be an expert in everything. Use 80/20. Use your best judgment about which 20% will have the greatest impact and focus your research there. For almost all businesses, competition has the biggest effect. In today's environment, the balance is often a mix of government, economy, and technology.

Can any of the uncontrollables be influenced? If it does involve the government, politics, or the law, can the refs be worked? If they can be worked, how?

We can't control a lot of things, but we can be informed about some of them.

Know the Game

Knowing the game consists of understanding the following.

- The history
- The language
- The rules
- The math

- Luck
- The moves

Some of this can be presented linearly. For example, we will discuss betting under "language," but it could be delayed until the "moves" section. The following pages are heavy on poker. They illustrate how some of the best play, but more importantly you should be able to see how the plays are transferable to business thinking.

The History

Every game, every industry, every business has a history. Poker probably comes from the French word *poque*, which means "to bluff." It was invented around 1834 in the New Orleans area. It worked its way up the Mississippi on riverboats and then spread to the Wild West. At one time, almost every western town had a saloon with a poker table in it. Shows our ancestors weren't wasting their time. Around 1920, the poker variation of Hold'em was, as you might expect, created in Texas.

Your industry association should provide a one-hour history seminar for all those new to the industry. This annually updated history session should be posted on its website.

The Language

Ever notice that, when you get a bunch of people together who work in the same industry, they start using words no one else understands? If you are a CEO who doesn't play poker, I have used language you don't comprehend. If you are a poker player without business experience, you have the same problem.

All of us must first learn the precise vocabulary of the game we are playing so we can *speak* in the same native language. Then, and far more importantly, we must constantly immerse ourselves in the game so we *think* in the same native language.

Betting is the real language of the poker table. You are telling everyone you have the best hand, are on a draw, or perhaps are deceiving them. This is public information, available for everyone to interpret. A lot of the discussion on betting also applies to a later section on moves. After all, every bet you make is a move.

Investing time, talent, and treasure is the language of business. Acquisitions, media buys, logistical networks, and other investments are, for the most part, information available to your competitors.

Aggressive betting usually pays off. Raising is much better than limping.

When you bet, you have two ways to win the hand. First, you really might have the best hand. Second, your opponents might fold. When you call, you have only one way to win the hand; you must be the best. Anytime you know you are going to call and are first to act, bet. You are giving yourself the two chances to win. If you get raised, you have more information, and you can then decide to either continue or fold.

When you have AA or KK, you are taught to thin the herd so you don't have many opponents on the flop, hopefully only one or at most two. The way to thin the herd is to bet strong, raise, and reraise preflop.

One successful business strategy is to do the same when you are sure you have a winner, at least at the start. When you invest so much during a launch, you create a high barrier for competitors.

One strategy used often is to get in there first. General Electric has a strategy of pre-empting emerging global markets by developing products in those markets. You really might have the best product, or your competitors might fold. Either way you win. If a competitor jumps in, at least you have more information, and you can decide to either continue or abort.

Average players vary their bet size based on their hand. Big mistake. Some overbet when they are weak and underbet when they are strong. Others are just the opposite. With a few showdowns, you'll be able to figure out where the player falls. Great players seldom change their preflop raises but will do so based not on the strength of their cards but on the skill level or how tight or loose the remaining opponents play.

Confident in his postflop skills, against a lesser player the great player will raise a lesser amount than he normally would. Against another great player, the raise will be more, trying either to get him to fold or to define his opponent's hand better. If the remaining players are tight, a lower raise might get them to fold. Bet sizing is correct when your opponent does exactly what you want him to do. If you want him to fold, you bet enough to get him to fold. If you want him to call, you bet enough to get him to call. In either case, you need to know his range and tipping points.

Against lesser competitors, you need not invest much at the start. Your experience in the growth phase (your postflop skills) will help you to outmaneuver them. Against someone more experienced, your initial investment should be higher.

This situation often occurs in oligopolies: that is, when you have only a few firms in a market. The smaller firm will bet heavily by producing a large quantity of its new product accompanied by a price designed to capture market share. Toyota initially was known for lower price and average quality. It wanted to introduce a new high-quality prestige brand to compete with Cadillac. When Toyota's Lexus was first introduced in the United States, you could buy a Lexus at a substantial discount compared to a Cadillac.

Many players with high pocket pairs attempt to get preflop draws out and isolate one opponent, at most two. The result in most cases is winning a relatively small pot. Those who check or just call at a loose table with AA or KK preflop find their top pair cracked when a drawer catches. With pocket AA at a 10-handed table, if everyone stayed to the river, the AA would win only 30% of the time. Of course, not everyone would stay to the river, but you get the idea.

Similarly, if you bet, but not enough to price your opponents out, you allow drawers to catch and win the pot.

Your first use of resources should always be to protect your top products, your stars. If you have a star and meekly invest to protect that star, you invite several competitors to stay in the market. A competitor's marginal product with some improvements then has the chance for a market share breakthrough and will dislodge your star product into the problem-child quadrant.

Faced with decreasing European market share, Heineken decided to increase marketing expenditures and expand cost cutting to protect its star product. Protection is often accomplished via politics. In Jakarta, policies were put in place to keep foreign airlines from competing with those owned in Jakarta.

This will sound strange at first. You, and your opponents, can make the pot so big that it becomes mathematically correct for several to call all the way to the river. When that happens, often the river card delivers the pot to someone who was behind all the way.

If several competitors are going after the same market, that market will become so attractive that even a competitor with a weak product might stay in because the potential rewards are so high.

Consider new technologies such as Apple products and their competitors. New products require huge outlays for a company to research, develop, and produce. Apple might beat others to the market, yet competitors have already invested so much that few fold.

In limit or no-limit cash games, we don't give free cards with two or more others in the hand unless we are so far ahead we are hoping someone might catch something.

Gordon never gives free cards. Negreanu, up against a single tournament opponent, depending on the board, says free cards are acceptable. Remember in a tournament you are trying to protect your stack as opposed to your hand. Your stack is far more important than winning a single hand. Hellmuth can often go through several hundred players but never go all-in. He avoids coin flips, even though he knows he's favored. He is protecting his stack. Yes, you'll get outdrawn now and then. But even then, you'll get information. In most situations, if you are ahead on the flop, you'll still be ahead on the river. But most importantly, you will avoid big pot traps.

In business, a free card means information you or your competitor gets without having to expend resources (Reineke). If you are the chip leader, the business with the most resources, you don't give free information unless you know you have the hand (i.e., a superior product) and want others to catch up.

A defensive bet is used by the top players if they are out of position and must act first and know they are going to call an opponent's bet. It's an out-of-position small bet intended to keep the in-position opponent from making a larger bet. Let's suppose you believe if you check your opponent will probably bet $1,000, which you intend to call. Instead of checking and calling, what will happen if you bet something less into your opponent, say $700? Your opponent might fold, but even if that doesn't happen, most players freeze up when someone out of position bets into them, and if they are going to continue in the hand they just call. So what? By betting the $700 into the opponent, you have saved $300 to make the call. If the player raises, you probably fold.

The defensive bet is often used in negotiation when one side is forced to make its position known first. If you have done your homework and you know the other person wants $100,000 for the property, you offer $70,000. In business, a defensive bet can be more subtle, but make sure your competitors know you are betting.

Defensive bets are commonly used in both auctions and negotiations. There is a TV show in which the participants bid on storage lockers. No one gets to inspect everything in the locker thoroughly, but everyone gets to look at the contents from a distance. Very limited information. The more experienced bidder observes the rookies' betting patterns on other lockers, and when a locker comes up that the experienced bidder wants, he bids a lesser amount than he knows the rookie would.

When quartz watches came out, mechanical watch manufacturers faced the threat of extinction. Before deciding to call by competing with their own quartz offerings or fold, they did some market research. They found that digital watches opened up a new target market, those who needed to "know how things tick." These companies essentially made a subtle defensive bet by producing see-through watches that exposed the gears and intricacies. The result was that mechanical watches are still made today (Rosenblatt).

When you have a monster, you get your chips in slowly during each round of betting, with as many (preferably all) in as possible by the end of the hand. The raises are kept small enough that you invite a call. If your raise is too big, your opponent might do the worst thing possible for you: fold. Say there's a 50%–70% pot size bet on the flop, followed by a pot-building bet on the turn and river. On the river, get as much value as you think you can extract.

> *Figuring out how to price things to best give yourself maximum value is . . . exactly what you do in a poker hand, and it's exactly what you do when you're trying to sell something in business.* — Daniel Negreanu

If you have created a product far superior to that of your competitor, consider allowing him to help develop the market for you, and then roll out your advanced product. You want competitors to throw money into the market. In poker, this is a perfect play. In business, you risk "the first to the market wins"; however, if your product really is untouchable, there's no reason not to let him do the betting for you. Let your competitor create market awareness through his bet of advertising; then capture the market with your superior offering.

Samsung has the resources to be the initial market leader but prefers to let others develop the market. Once it is sure of a true market trend, it makes its move to be the market leader.

As we have discussed, customers and opponents have tipping points. The point where, if the bet is too high, they will fold or, if the price is too high, they won't buy. When someone with a unique product asks for pricing advice, I flippantly say, "Keep raising your price until everyone stops buying." If you could find a cure for the cold, you'd need to find out what it's worth to your customers as opposed to how much it costs you to produce it. In a one-on-one negotiation, knowing how much the other person can afford and what it's worth to him are two strategic tipping points.

To the experienced pro, a bet of a relatively small percentage of the pot on the river is read as either a value bet or a bluff (known as a post oak bluff). Unfortunately, he seldom knows which. Many pros call because they believe their opponent is trying to make a move on them.

The value bet is often used in negotiation, usually after there is agreement on the main point or when the deal is almost done. It consists of asking for a few additional provisions, extra concessions, when everyone is in a "yes" mode.

I don't like it when someone welches. That's when I definitely bet for value.

I had won a substantial judgment, far in excess of what it was really worth, because the defendant didn't show up in court. We got together and agreed on what I considered to be a fair settlement. When it got to signing, he wanted to change the deal. Okay, if you want to renegotiate, we'll renegotiate. I went through every page of the proposed deal and increased everything in my favor. Then I told him if he didn't sign I would collect the judgment. He signed.

In no-limit, unless the pro is short stacked and wants to get to the flop as cheaply as possible, if he is first to act, he will raise. It takes a better hand to call a raise than to make a raise. This is known as the gap principle (Sklansky). If you have a good product, you can certainly enter the market first. But if a competitor has introduced a strong product accompanied by a major investment, you must have either a superior or a potentially superior product to enter the market. This concept is closely related to whether a business is known for making the "first move" or intentionally waiting for the "second move." Whether a company is one or the other depends on what the CEO is most comfortable with.

Notice how Walmart, with its internal mantra "Where we're not, what we're not," is often the first with a new product or service, such as low-price prescription drugs. Target watches to see whether Walmart's experiments are successful before it enters a similar market. Apple is also known for making the first move, such as with its entry into digital music. Others wait to see if the market accepts the concept before staking out a competitive position. Each strategy has pros and cons. The first move is great when it works, expensive when it doesn't. The second move costs less to develop a product but more to outmarket the company that makes the first move.

Value and bluff bets are the same percentage of the pot, so your opponent can't figure out which is which. The only time you should consider increasing the size of your value bet is when your lone opponent is more skilled or an aggressive-loose. An overbet will look bluffy to both. The more skilled reasons that a big bet is a bluff that he'd employ. The aggressive-loose is a bluffer and thinks everyone is bluffing him. You might get a very profitable call.

In the battle for portable music, Apple overbet when it developed its own device and was first to market. Although the device wasn't perfected, Apple knew it needed to lead in an innovative market. Microsoft followed later with its own product, thinking it could pick up market share. Apple's overbet drew a call from Microsoft, one that contributed to overall market growth. We've certainly all heard of the iPod, but does anyone remember the Zune (Rosenblatt)?

If all you do is call when you have correct pot odds, any tough opponent will pick up on this. Regardless of his cards, he will bet enough to constantly give you a negative expected value (discussed in detail in a few pages) and push you out of the pot. Knowing pot odds is absolutely essential when you have raised and he goes all-in. In a cash game with a positive expected value, the decision is clear. In a tournament, though a call might be mathematically correct, the best players will weigh that against being eliminated.

A competitor who knows you stay with a product by just matching his investment might be smart enough to know that, if he substantially increases his investment in market penetration or product development, you might abandon yours. When deciding what to do with the fledgling competitor who puts all of his company's resources into one basket, a careful analysis of your potential ROI leads you to decide whether to continue or abandon.

The executive at Microsoft who recognized that its Zune music wasn't going to make it saved the company millions.

Nut flushes, obvious to even the average player, often don't pay much, if any. Connectors, with a sequenced board, are also obvious.

Some hands, such as T7 suited (Negreanu's favorite), when they catch, especially with the hidden straight, pay off big time. Opponents with a set, two pair, or even an overpair just can't let go of their hands.

Hands such as AK, when they catch, usually result in a small pot won, if they win. Even AA usually doesn't win a big pot.

If you launch only great products, no one will help you to build the market. Yes, you will essentially have a short-term monopoly, but your market development costs will be high.

With experience, you must play hands such as T7s, products that look like they don't have a lot of potential at the beginning. Several competitors might have better hands than you at the start, and they grow the market, so if your product does pan out, market acceptance (the pot) has been built mostly by your competitors.

The better your cards, the less aggressively you bet. You want to keep your opponents contributing to the pot. Please don't throw me into the briar patch.

The greater your resources, the better the combination of your product, price, place, promotion, and people, the more you want to let your competitors develop the market.

The Rules

Nesson emphasizes to his young lawyers to be "players of the game rather than appliers of the rules." However, before you can play, you must know the rules, both written and unwritten, which rules are enforced and which are not, when they are symmetrical or not, who interprets the rules, when they force you out of the game, when the rules can be changed, and when they can be used to your advantage.

It's a lot easier to play the game when everyone has a written set of consistent rules. Sounds simple enough, but you should assume nothing about the rules.

Business rules vary from state to state, country to country, and person to person. Sometimes no one really seems to know the rules. If you call the IRS multiple times with the same question, you'll get multiple answers. Some just aren't sure how to interpret the rules, and others interpret the rules to suit themselves.

There are many unwritten poker rules, usually involving courtesy (but ignored online).

When my Chicago bank thought it needed to pad my loan so I could pay off local government officials, it was more than surprised when I said you don't have to bribe anyone in La Crosse, Wisconsin.

Rules mean nothing if they aren't enforced. Some rules can be broken and often are. Sometimes it depends on who is in charge.

There is a rule in poker that you can't tell an opponent which cards you hold. Poker pro Jamie Gold, television producer, talent agent, and winner of the WSOP Main Event, would often tell his opponent what he had. A player who knew the rule would then act on the interpretation that Gold didn't hold the cards he'd mentioned. Gold, to my knowledge, has never had the dealer declare his hand dead for violating the rules.

When a lone opponent, the last to act at my riverboat casino, turned over his cards and then called, I asked for a ruling. They said his hand was dead. I used their obscure rule to my advantage to prove a point. I gave my opponent half the pot.

Despite years of notices from suspicious investors to the Securities and Exchange Commission, it sent a green attorney whose voice hadn't changed yet to talk to Madoff. He simply talked his way out of every inquiry. Andrew, Bernie's son, describes his dad as a "master manipulator" (Fishman).

It was obvious my opponent had lied several times during the deposition. I turned to my attorney and said, "We've got him on perjury." He said, "I don't know of a district attorney who would bring perjury charges or a judge who would find anyone guilty. People lie all the time, and no one cares. Besides, if people didn't commit perjury, we wouldn't need lawyers." That last part is a good thought.

So, not only do you have to know the rules, but you must also know which refs will enforce which rules.

In poker, the rules are symmetrical. In life, they are not. *They* use suicide bombers, *we* don't. In poker, you seldom see new rules, but that's not true in business.

Originally, Microsoft spent 100% of its time and resources on developing new products. Once it was sued by the justice department for giving away its software, it switched gears. Now it spends millions every year on lobbying. A complete waste.

Government knows best. Ha. The government syndrome says that more rules, laws, and regulations are the answer (Gratzner). Sarbanes-Oxley was supposed to prevent future Enrons and WorldComs. All it did was add another layer of legalese for board compliance. It did nothing to fix the real problem — the quality of people on boards. The Troubled Asset Relief Program (TARP) bailed out the failed financials that were Sarbanes-Oxley compliant. More rules, more costs, same old results (Pozen).

A good idea. Get rid of all the paper in hospitals and replace it with an individual electronic record for each patient. And then link the records worldwide. Here's where it got sticky. As opposed to letting the market decide whether it was a good idea or not, the government, with big-buck incentives, decided it would force hospitals to choose one of a few recently developed software systems and go paperless. How? First it told the hospital the government would reimburse it for the actual cost of the system. Then, in future years, it would penalize the hospital's reimbursement for Medicare and Medicaid if it didn't adopt one of the paperless systems.

One of our local hospitals decided that it had better comply. It looked good on paper. It would receive more than $23 million (the cost of the system) and save money in the future on Medicare and Medicaid reimbursements.

As the system was implemented, check-ins that used to take less than a minute went to 10 minutes. Long lines of patients. Physicians found they were spending far less time with the patient and much more time on the computer. Doctors accustomed to entering data in a few minutes on a previous electronic and paper system either tripled the time needed for entering it or found they couldn't enter what they wanted to. Others who'd had their medical assistants handle prescriptions and other documentation now found they had to spend time doing so on their own.

Why the chaos? Two reasons. First, the system was developed by some smart programmers with only minor input from doctors and no input from medical assistants and check-in personnel. The programmers focused on efficiency as opposed to effectiveness, but the program was neither efficient nor effective. The programmers were great at programming, but they didn't know much about how doctors really do doctoring. Second, and this was the big problem, the government got involved. If it hadn't decided to spend billions of our money on coercion, the medical market and our local hospital would have waited until they were sure everything worked. Now our hospital is scrambling, at an estimated cost of several millions, to make modifications so the system is more friendly to those who actually use it. And there is an unknown cost of seeing fewer patients. Where do those millions come from? Either the taxpayers or the patients.

In Wisconsin, if a school district wants to spend above the state-imposed cap, it must ask the voters via a referendum. The schools always schedule the referendum during an off-year minor election time, when the voter turnout will be only about 10%, and they can stack the deck by getting all the teachers and union members to vote.

You are not playing against the house, you are playing against opponents. The house wins whether or not you do because it takes a rake on each hand. The rake, when it's excessive in relation to pot size, is your enemy. This is why it's difficult to win at low-stakes limit casino tables. The rake, at higher-stakes games, is much less percentagewise, so it's easier to show a profit. Smart players avoid playing where the rake is just too much. Taxes are the businessman's rake.

In poker sometimes, there's an additional rake for the bad beat. In business, there's an insidious hidden rake. It's the extra work complying with government-required reports and paperwork. This is work your staff — whom you pay — do for the government. And at least a quarter of your managers' time will be spent trying to avoid lawsuits.

> *The United States has less than five percent of the world's population but two-thirds of the world's attorneys.*

Our legislators are mostly lawyers, and they continually add new laws without bright lines. The employer must provide reasonable accommodation to those with a handicap provided the accommodation doesn't impose a hardship on the company. That's the Americans with Disabilities Act. What does it mean? They ought to rename it the "Lawyers' Full Employment Act." Congress has taken the Ten Commandments beyond absurdity. If I could pass a law, it would be that for every new law, three existing laws must be eliminated.

At least with poker the bad beat rake is largely paid out to the players. In business, it's never paid out to you; rather, it's paid out to government employees and society's takers.

When taxes, government regulations, or hours spent on lawsuit avoidance are excessive, they are your enemy. You are better off moving to another state or country or closing the business down.

There are very few companies that put the U.S. worker above profit. Frank Uhler, former CEO of La Crosse Footwear, could have made several more millions had his products been made in Mexico. He flat out said he'd be dead before the company would ever outsource anything since he was "committed to providing jobs for Americans." After he passed away, the products were outsourced, the La Crosse plant closed, and hundreds lost their jobs.

Other American companies, while preferring to stay in the United States, have been forced financially, yes forced, to move overseas. Our corporate tax rate is much higher than those in countries such as Switzerland and Ireland. Trying to stay ahead of our changing tax laws, first they move their headquarters, then their patents, then their research and development, and finally their manufacturing. And they aren't just small companies. Look overseas and you'll see substantial operations with hundreds of companies such as Pfizer, Merck, Google, and General Electric. Today U.S. companies have over $1 trillion in profits permanently sequestered overseas because our tax laws penalize them if they bring that money back to America. Black & Decker, Converse, Levi's, and even Barbie, all once U.S. icons, have all moved overseas.

A side comment. There are only two ends to the tax food chain — the government and the individual. Businesses are not tax payers, they are tax collectors. When a business gets hit with a higher cost of materials, it raises its price. When it is faced with a higher tax, it raises its price. A business that absorbs an increase in taxes or the cost of materials will eventually go out of business. The consumer pays for increased business taxes by paying higher prices. The consumer also pays for all of the hidden time spent on lawsuit avoidance and compliance with government paperwork. When a politician says "Corporations should pay their fair share of taxes," I hear "Consumers, you are too stupid to know you are going to pay more, so I can get your votes by bribing you with your own money."

Blinds and antes are forced bets. If there were no blinds and antes, no one would ever play unless he was dealt AA. Tournament play is a fight for the blinds and antes. When you get to the point that antes are significant, if you are going to enter a preflop pot, do so strongly and try to pick up the antes immediately.

When the government forces you to buy car insurance, health insurance, or any form of insurance, these are forced bets. A permit is a forced bet. Paying off the inspector is a forced bet. Just trying to keep up with all the laws is a forced bet. In the United States, the most insidious and hidden forced bet is the shrinking value of the dollar.

In a tournament, the blinds and antes escalate with time. This is the same as inflation in business, where projections must take into account increased future costs.

No poker player would ever get into a game in which the house could, in the middle of a hand, declare deuces wild.

Arch Coal invested $250 million for a permit for a mine in West Virginia. After years of careful review, the Army Corps of Engineers approved the permit. With a new administration in office, the Environmental Protection Agency then revoked the permit. Hundreds of jobs and a quarter of a billion down the drain.

Businesses need to trust that the rules of the game will stay relatively stable. We should never make long-term investments with an uncertain government in power that might impose dramatic new regulations, increase taxes, or create unfair advantages for competitors. Individuals and businesses adjust to the rules, although individuals are more nimble. When online sites were closed down in the United States by the Department of Justice, avid online players either moved to Canada or transitioned to live play.

When one organization is harmed by a change in the rules, it often creates opportunities for others. When the Canadian government ruled that over-the-counter medicine couldn't be given to children under six, it created a market for natural cold medicine companies to jump in (Eike).

The Math

Part of poker is pure math. The universe is all math. Math can lead you to conclusions you never thought of. It can illuminate hidden realities. Understanding and interpreting numbers, data, statistics, and probabilities are essential in both poker and business. In this respect, poker is easier than business. As you and your staff construct decision trees and assign probabilities and weights, they are not exact. They are best guesses. No matter how good your guess, it becomes more complicated and more difficult to predict when people are involved.

If we play a game with perfect information, such as chess, we can rely completely on the math. But in life we never have perfect information. Here we need the math, but we should never make a decision based solely on the numbers.

Expected value doesn't mean we are going to win the hand. It means over the long run, if we play the hand thousands of times, we will come out ahead if the expected value is positive and behind if it's negative.

One question I often get asked is this: if the probability of catching specific cards doesn't change, why must we have a certain number of bets to stay in a hand? First review the expected value (EV) equation.

EV = (probability of winning)(pot size) − (probability of losing)(amount of your call)

Now let's go through an example. Suppose we have a four flush on the flop. What's our probability of catching?

Probability of catching = $\dfrac{\text{Number of cards left in the deck to make the flush}}{\text{Number of cards we don't know}}$

$= (13 - 4)/47 = 0.19$

Probability of not catching = 1.00 – Probability of catching
$= 1.00 - 0.19 = 0.81$

So far we know several parts of the EV equation.

EV = (0.19)(pot size) – (0.81) (amount of your call)

And, to illustrate the point, we'll just use number of bets (e.g., one bet could be $100, two bets $200, and so on) for both pot size and amount of your call. If the pot had three bets and you must call one bet, here's the equation.

EV = (0.19)(3) – (0.81)(1)
= -0.24 bets

A negative EV, -0.24 bets, means that if we played this hand with this size of pot several thousand times, we would, over the long run, lose an average of 0.24 bets for every hand played. Not a good deal.

How about four bets in the pot?

EV = (0.19)(4) – (0.81)(1)
= -0.05 bets

The EV is still negative. Not good. We need a positive EV.

How about five bets in the pot?

EV = (0.19)(5) – (0.81)(1)
= +0.14 bets

All right. A positive expected value.
How about six bets in the pot?

$$EV = (0.19)(6) - (0.81)(1)$$
$$= +0.33 \text{ bets}$$

What has changed? Has the probability of getting the flush card changed? No. The probability is the same. The only change is the amount in the pot, and that in turn changes the expected value.

In business, we can use game theory, decision trees, probabilities, expected value, operations research, and other forms of mathematical analysis. In some cases, these are necessary but in no way sufficient.

We can't really know the probabilities associated with each branch. It's our best guess, and that's all it is. And, once people are involved, unforeseen branches pop up out of nowhere. We don't know what we don't know.

The pot is offering you 4:1, said as "four to one." It means you are putting in one dollar to get four dollars. This is the same thing as return on investment. Your ROI in this case is a mere 400%.

In poker, pot odds are compared with something called hand odds. Hand odds are your probability of making your hand when you are drawing. If your pot odds (what the pot is offering you) are greater than your hand odds (the probability of making your hand), you have a positive EV, and it is mathematically correct to call; if not, fold.

It's not quite as easy to determine when making a business investment, but still we need our financial wizards to determine our pot odds (what our ROI will probably be) and compare it to our probability of being successful (making our hand) to see if we should continue or fold.

This is a common practice in business when forecasting capital budgets. Probabilities are assigned to various outcomes, or Monte Carlo simulations are run for a distribution of possible outcomes, resulting in a calculation of net present value or internal rate of return.

Often, in a low-limit game, someone in early position will limp preflop, starting a cascading effect, resulting in several callers. If there are several limpers in a pot, it obviously gets bigger. But the investment required to stay in the pot doesn't increase. That's why you see a professional on the button call with almost any two cards with several limpers. Either he will catch something or, if almost everyone checks on the flop, he will bluff on the flop or isolate one player and continue with a strong play on the turn.

The same thing happens with a low-cost product. One company invests a minimal amount, followed by several competitors essentially calling the first company. With several competitors investing something but not enough to individually capture the market, that delay provides an opportunity to come in late, even though your product might not look strong.

Even with the initial success of MySpace, social networking competitors such as vMix, Wayn, Xanga, and Facebook called with offerings of their own. None looked strong at the start, but Facebook took off and displaced MySpace.

In poker, the best player will look into the future beyond just seeing the turn card to see how much more he'll probably make: that is, the future bets or calls of opponents on the river, if he makes his hand. Using pot odds alone might dictate that a player should fold, but using implied odds keeps him in the hand. Many no-limit hands depend on implied odds.

Implied odds are greater the stronger your opponent's hand and lesser the weaker his hand. If he has a strong product, he'll continue to build the market and pay off a big bet on the river. As always, the greats know in advance how much they will bet, raise, or reraise on the river if they catch, and they base that bet on how strong they think their opponent's hand is.

How much more, if any, can we make if the market turns out to be much greater than it is today? How much more will our competitors put into expanding the market?

When a company spends $150 million to create a product that sells for a few hundred dollars (Apple and iPhone), it's betting heavily on the implied odds of market acceptance. Pharmaceutical companies spend billions on R & D because they know if they hit a good product, the implied odds — because of both a patent and a built-in revenue stream — are exceptional.

In game theory, there's a classic case of the prisoner's dilemma. Bonnie and Clyde are caught after an attempted bank robbery. They are placed in separate cells and cannot communicate with each other. If they don't confess, the sheriff can only prove illegal possession of a firearm, resulting in one year in jail. If one doesn't talk but the other does, the one who confesses (as a witness for the prosecution) gets out free, but the other gets ten years. If they both confess, they both get five years. Their best outcome is if they can collude and neither confesses. If each turns the other in, the result is bad for both. A lesson from this game is that, when everyone acts in his own self-interest, often the results aren't nearly as good as when he cooperates. Less Adam Smith and more Keynes.

Many years ago the top scientific brains were asked to come up with a program that would result in the most wins when playing the prisoners' dilemma thousands of times against all other programs. The one that won was a simple two-liner. The first round Clyde would be nice and not turn in Bonnie. If she didn't turn in Clyde, then the next round he wouldn't turn in Bonnie. If Bonnie turned in Clyde, then the next round he would retaliate and turn in Bonnie. If she didn't turn in Clyde the round after that, then he wouldn't turn in Bonnie. And so on. This tit-for-tat program resulted in the highest score of all programs submitted. The lesson: start off being nice. Continue to be nice as long as your opponent is nice. As soon as your opponent becomes negative, you respond in kind. And continue to respond in kind regardless of what your opponent does. This two-line model works well in all forms of life. When Gadhafi attacked us, Reagan responded in kind. When he backed down, so did we. Gadhafi then understood what would happen if he attacked us again. This concept of reciprocity is known by the world's best leaders. A favor here is returned by a favor there.

This solution is essentially calling. I prefer to raise with a non-proportional response. If someone is nice to me, I will be extremely nice to him. If someone is not nice to me, look out. Israelis have tried both calling and raising approaches to rocket attacks. Raising works better.

Although some people cling to absolute answers, there are some real disadvantages of game theory. It says players are always rational. Not always true. Often we see divorces become irrational. It assumes payoffs are given. Seldom true. Sometimes they are very difficult to measure, especially when we are trying to measure utility (i.e., what the outcome is worth to the player). Different players have different utilities — different preferences. We will discuss the important concept of payoffs shortly. Game theory also doesn't take into account the type of play an opponent prefers. This is why we must know our opponent; we can then adjust according to his tendencies. And it doesn't take into account that you might be more clever than he is or, worse, that he is more clever than you are.

| number of opponents left in the hand preflop | | | | | | | | | |
you hold unsuited	1	2	3	4	5	6	7	8	9
AK	6%	12%	18%	24%	30%	36%	42%	48%	
AQ	7%	14%	21%	28%	35%	42%	49%		
AJ	8%	16%	24%	32%	40%	48%			
AT	9%	18%	27%	36%	45%				
A9	10%	20%	30%	40%	50%				
A8	11%	22%	33%	44%					
A7	12%	24%	36%	48%					
A6	13%	26%	39%						
A5	14%	28%	42%						
A4	15%	30%	45%						
A3	16%	32%	48%						
A2	17%	34%							

Figure 3.11 Probability of at least one opponent having a better hand when you have A-x off suit

Average players play Ace-anything off-suit. Is this a good tactic? The far-left-hand column in Figure 3.11 shows our hero holding AK off-suit all the way down to A2. The row across the top indicates the number of players left in the preflop hand. The figure shows the probability of any remaining opponent holding an Ace with a higher kicker, an Ace with the same kicker but suited, or a pocket pair. Those parts of the table not shown indicate the probability that at least one opponent has a better starting hand. Of particular interest is when you hold AK off-suit under the gun at a 10-handed table; someone else is usually ahead of you preflop. Even though that's what the math says, I don't know of many players, professional or otherwise, who fold AK in early position.

How about calling a preflop all-in with AK? Other than a short stack all-in, the bettor usually has a pocket pair. What do you do with AK? Although your all-in opponent is favored, unless he has AA or KK, against any pair you'll win approximately 44% of the time (43% against QQ, JJ, TT since those pairs take away your chance of making a straight by one percent). But if one player goes all-in, and another person calls, and you have AK, you have to consider the likelihood that one of the two players has one of your outs, probably an Ace. If one of your outs is gone, then you have only a 33% chance of beating a pocket pair.

On the flip side, math can inspire great decisions. Any two cards against AK will win a third of the time or more. Even 72 will beat AA 12% of the time, much better odds than when George Washington wrote, on 14 January 1776, "Few people know the predicament we are in."

When a match is down to heads up, you'll notice the smart pro with a substantial chip lead over the small stack will go all-in on almost every hand. He knows that, even if he lets that small stack double up a few times, conditional probability is on his side.

I often go through this concept with my students using roulette as an example. If you bet $2 on black and it comes up black, you get your $2 back plus another $2. We'll assume you let it ride on black. If you lose, you double your previous bet until you win. Let's suppose you bet $2 and lost. Your next bet is $4. You lose, so your next bet is $8. You lose again, so your next bet is $16. Then $32. Then $64. Then $128. Then $256. Now you finally win. If you add up how much you spent from your very first loss, you'll find that you spent a total of $254. Your net gain for this series of transactions is $2, the amount of your original bet. You then start all over again with a $2 bet and keep doubling up each time you lose until you finally win. Can you lose doing this? Of course, since every event is independent of each other event, and it certainly could come up red nine times in a row, but it illustrates the concept of trying to use conditional probability to your advantage.

A McKinsey & Company study found that, if companies increased prices by just one percent and demand remained constant, operating profits would increase on average by 11% (Macht).

A few years ago General Electric did some research in China and discovered that 90% of the population either had no access to modern health care or could not afford it. To the upper 10% of the market, GE introduced its ultrasound machine, which was large, immobile, and expensive to use. Over a billion people represented the other 90% of the market. They needed a portable product that could travel to remote areas and perform similar functions. This inspired GE to create a new business model. It hired local Chinese engineers to see if they could solve the problem for the bulk of the market. The engineers developed a laptop device with a probe attached to it. They produced it at 15% of the cost and sacrificed only 50% of the performance. Aside from being a less expensive and more portable ultrasound that could fit into a backpack, the new device could be used during many emergency situations (Rosenblatt).

```
10 handed                          AA
                              AKs  KK  AK
                         KQs  AQs  QQ  AQ  KQ
                    QJs  KJs  AJs  JJ  AJ  KJ  QJ
                JTs QTs KTs   ATs  TT  AT  KT  QT  JT
            T9s J9s Q9s K9s   A9s  99
        98s T8s J8s Q8s K8s   A8s  88
    87s 97s T7s J7s Q7s K7s   A7s  77
 76s 86s 96s         Q6s K6s  A6s  66
 65s 75s 85s         Q5s K5s  A5s  55
54s 64s 74s          Q4s K4s  A4s  44
53s                  Q3s K3s  A3s  33
                     Q2s K2s  A2s  22


6 handed                           AA
                              AKs  KK  AK
                         KQs  AQs  QQ  AQ  KQ
                    QJs  KJs  AJs  JJ  AJ  KJ  QJ
                JTs QTs KTs   ATs  TT  AT  KT  QT  JT
            T9s J9s Q9s K9s   A9s  99
        98s T8s J8s Q8s K8s   A8s  88
    87s 97s T7s J7s Q7s K7s   A7s  77
                     Q6s K6s  A6s  66
                         K5s  A5s  55
                         K4s  A4s  44
                         K3s  A3s
                              A2s


3 handed                           AA
                              AKs  KK  AK
                         KQs  AQs  QQ  AQ  KQ
                    QJs  KJs  AJs  JJ  AJ  KJ  QJ
                JTs QTs KTs   ATs  TT  AT  KT  QT  JT
            T9s J9s Q9s K9s   A9s  99  A9  K9
            T8s J8s Q8s K8s   A8s  88  A8  K8
                         K7s  A7s  77  A7  K7
                         K6s  A6s  66  A6
                         K5s  A5s  55  A5
                         K4s  A4s  44  A4
                              A3s
                              A2s
```

Figure 3.12 Math Experts Disagree

Math can guide you to correct decisions, but don't let it be the sole guide. When you get five economists in a room, you'll get at least six different opinions. Mathematicians aren't as bad, but not all understanding is equal.

Figure 3.12 shows which preflop hands, depending on how many players are dealt cards at an extremely loose table, have a positive expectation. Some of the best poker mathematicians in the world disagree, for they believe it's the number left in the hand, not the number of players dealt cards, that is the determining factor. Their thinking would be correct if it were a pure expectation calculation, because the cards for the players who have folded are unknown. But their analysis doesn't take into account which cards have likely been removed from play by those who have folded. Suppose, for example, at a very loose full-ring table, the first four to act preflop fold. In a 52-card universe, eight cards are gone. In all likelihood, no Aces were folded, which means the probability of someone remaining with an Ace has increased.

The point? The math is helpful but not always as precise as the math guy tells you. You need to know the math, but you don't want to be known as a pure math player.

Luck

Sexton has testified in court that he believes poker is 70% skill, 30% luck. Ferguson puts them equally at 50%.

Part of the skill is with the math. This part of the thinking of players leads them to make a decision based on whether their hand odds (the probability of success based on the number of outs) are greater than their pot odds (the investment that needs to be made compared to how much they might win). In other words, is their expected value positive or negative? They put themselves in positive expectations and avoid negative ones.

The average player doesn't even think of pot odds. He relies on emotion and intuition. His brain is looking for opium receptors with a dopamine and serotonin rush with the big payoff if he catches a card. When he fills his inside straight or a set of twos on the river, he thinks he made the right play. He's invincible. When a great player takes a big loss in such a situation, he gives thanks because he knows he has an opponent who will eventually lose all of his chips.

All great players know they can control the decision but not the outcome. Gordon: "I get my money in with the best hand, and that is really all you can do." They get their money in good. Every player has suffered many a bad beat. Luck always plays a part in the outcome. But the great players know they reduce the luck factor by aggressively putting themselves in positive expectation situations.

Every stock market investor has placed his money in a company whose sales and profits increased but with only lackluster stock appreciation. The PETCO San Diego Padres ballpark has helped local development, but the taxpayer is still on the hook for millions. Apple has had great products such as OpenDoc, Cyberdog, and Newton, but all failed.

We must all follow the great players. Get our money in good. Keep ourselves and our businesses in positive expectation situations and avoid negative ones.

Every other Wednesday I play a small stakes, full-ring limit game with physicians. Everyone must ante. No one folds preflop. Good pot odds for almost any two cards. We could save a lot of time by having everyone put in his ante and preflop bet and just go directly to the flop.

This is strictly best-hand poker. I'm one of the few who might fold preflop or on the flop, and by the river almost every pot is huge.

Unlike most games, where whoever is ahead on the flop often wins the showdown, the person ahead on the flop wins fewer showdowns than he would in a normal game. Of course, the miracle card comes more frequently since there are at least four players left on the river. This game is 95% luck, five percent skill (the only real skill is knowing when to fold), but their company is more than worth it.

If you are up against competitors for whom the financial investment is small, and the return on the investment is potentially high, the ability to apply superior business skill is reduced. The market winner can easily be one whose product just got lucky.

Sometimes products are the result of luck. During World War II, rubber became scarce in the United States as Japan invaded rubber-producing countries. The government asked American inventors to develop synthetic rubber to produce tires. One inventor, James Wright, tried but failed. His product bounced but couldn't be used as a rubber substitute. Several years later, a toy store owner saw the product, and Silly Putty was on its way.

The law of large numbers can't be repealed. Averages will turn out to be average. But, in the short run, things don't work on average much of the time. They come in clumps. Clumps of positive expectations pay off one after another, and we think we are brilliant. In poker, you'll hear the term "running good." Associated with each of the 169 starting hands is a mathematical expectation. When a player wins more than he theoretically should, he is said to be running good. Defying poker or business gravity doesn't last for long.

"Running bad" means he wins less than mathematically expected. Clumps of positive expectations don't pay off, and we question our decisions. Short-run disasters can be longer than you thought possible. A sign of a great poker or business player is not how much he wins with his good luck clumps, but how he handles his losses with his bad luck clumps. He knows that, if he hangs in there, putting himself in positive situations, in the long run, if he doesn't die first, he will come out ahead. "I am playing my A game, consistently, relentlessly, tirelessly."

All the poker greats put luck on their side by being as prepared as possible when an opening presents itself. They use all the elements we will discuss to make the best decision possible. When opportunity knocks, it's too late to figure out how to open the door. Most luck is where preparation meets opportunity.

Chuck was no longer playing on the tour. He became a teaching pro in Columbus. The senior tour was in town. Chuck helped the players to warm up and returned later to watch the matches. Tennis great Bjorn Borg's opponent was injured. Chuck was in the stands, still wearing his tennis clothes, when the tournament director called to him and said, "We have 5,000 people in the stands. They paid to see a match. Get out on the court. You're playing Borg."

Borg had always been his hero. But they'd never met before that day. Chuck didn't have a racquet and asked Borg if he could use one of his.

Luck had nothing to do with Chuck's once-in-a-lifetime opportunity. Chuck won.

The Moves

Good cards at the start of a hand are likely to be good cards at the end. Good preflop decisions make for good postflop decisions. Bad preflop decisions make for poor postflop decisions. In for a dime, in for a dollar.

You'll never have as much control over a situation as you do at the beginning. And, as with many decisions, both big and small, this is zero or one. Either you're in the hand or you're not. Either you make a small investment or you don't. Either you hire or you don't. Either you marry her or you don't. Keri Russell: "Sometimes it's the smallest decision that can change your life forever." Your personal, business, or national history often turns on a dime. As Jack David said as he was looking over my first draft, "This applies very well to publishing. Accept good manuscripts, and things are more likely to turn out good."

When I'm working with students who are learning poker, before they look at their hole cards, I make them say to themselves, "Money saved is money earned." The point is that beginners tend to play way too many marginal hands and slowly bleed away their chips. As they learn, they must understand that every bet they don't make is the same as a bet they won. I make them start off with premium hands: that is, tight play. This requires a great deal of patience and discipline since premium hands don't come along often. They might sit at the table for over an hour and not play one hand.

Likewise, substantial business investments shouldn't be made by rookies. It takes a doctor 250 times doing a procedure before he is said to be proficient at it. You don't want to be among the first 250. When I was in the Army, I thought it would be a good idea to get my wisdom teeth out since it wouldn't cost me anything. The older dentist stood looking into my mouth while the younger one hammered one of my back teeth with a chisel. The older one said, "No, no, no. That's not the way."

If you are in the hand, a small investment can easily turn into a big one. Once the new guy is hired, valuable resources are spent on guidance, training, and education. Small, seemingly inconsequential decisions cascade into more time, talent, and treasure. This is fine if the initial binary decision was a good one, terrible if it wasn't.

It was a fateful day when Nam Youg, former CEO of LG Electronics, decided to put all of his phone eggs into Microsoft's basket. Windows

Mobile turned out to be less than the operating system LG needed, resulting in decreased market share and substantial losses.

An error uncorrected becomes a mistake. A mistake uncorrected becomes a problem. A problem uncorrected becomes a dilemma. A dilemma uncorrected becomes a crisis.

> *Take two people with equal intelligence, the one with the most information wins.*
>
> *— W.R. Grace*

I'd rather have position than cards (Cline). Position is power. Why? You get more information on which to make a decision. With position, you get free cards. You control the hand. You control the size of the pot. You can bet for value. You risk fewer chips. You play more hands. You can bluff more. You win most of your chips with position. The out-of-position opponent who bets is putting more of his money at risk while you can decide if you are going to play or fold. Which leads to the most important position statement: if you play yourself, you'll always win more money in position than out of position. Position is crucial in both high-stakes and short-handed games, especially for the superior player. When you have position, turn up the heat, especially at the first sign of weakness.

> *In a cash game, when you have more than three or four players in the pot, when I have the button, I'll call with any two cards about 90% of the time. The button is so strong in no-limit Hold'em. You can pick up a pot with any two cards. — Kirk Morrison, WSOP champion*

When you are out of position, you have to do most of the guessing. You don't know what your opponent will do. You must rely on card strength. You have to avoid playing big pots. You don't get free cards. Unless you bet out, perhaps with a defensive bet, or counter with a check-raise, you don't have control. You risk more money than someone in position. If you play yourself out of position, you'll always win less than if you are in position. In the military, you must respect rank even if you don't respect the person; in poker, you must respect position even if you don't respect the opponent. In tournaments, if you are playing a hand out of position, be careful. Very careful.

The best place to be in a hand is the last to act. The second best is the first to enter the pot, where you can force your opponent to make a tough decision.

You want to be either the first to enter the market or the last. If you are first, you can keep the competition out with a large investment. But first to market involves a high degree of risk, and last is often better. You get to see what your competitors have developed and how much they have invested in developing the market.

Recalling the Boston Consulting Group Matrix discussed earlier, you have the best position with your star products and the worst position with your dogs (Fritz).

Lewis Lehr, CEO of 3M: "The secret, if there is one, is to dump the flops as soon as they are recognized." Although he is talking about product flops, the parallel is the same (Collins and Porass). Folding is an essential skill in both poker and business. It's fundamental to success.

If you fold preflop, you have lost nothing (other than a possible blind or ante). If you fold on the flop, you have lost a minor investment. In operations research, we use linear programming to figure out a theoretical maximum (win) and minimum (loss). We always want to lose the least with our bad hands. Of course, with position, you'll always make the most or lose the least.

Maybe you underestimated the competition or overestimated the market potential. Perhaps you simply invested too much in a bad idea. Sometimes it's best to realize you've made a mistake and bow out gracefully.

The government is the only player I know who keeps playing bad hands and survives. Businesses can't. Poker players can't. That individual in your organization who says "Close this division" might be saving you from continuing in a bad hand. Although criticized at the time, Ford's decision to discontinue the Mercury brand proved to be a smart move (Nighbor).

The majority of the time, when the best players play a big pot, they have a big hand or the makings of a big hand. Despite what you see on television, the great players bluff a lot less than it appears. You are watching an edited show, and the producers are going to show you the most exciting hands. Those hands often involve bluffing.

Knowing your opponents is the key to bluffing. Good, solid, tight players can be bluffed. They know they are supposed to fold. Passive-loose players can't be bluffed. They are the ones calling you on the river because they "want to keep you honest."

I'll try a bluff on the flop with a continuation bet against one or two opponents. On the turn, if I don't catch, I will usually give up. Players superior to me will continue by firing a second and sometimes third barrel.

One signal of a bluff is when the bettor's bet size has increased. Most greats interpret that bet as a bluff. An outrageous demand in the middle of a negotiation is often perceived by the experienced negotiator as a bluff.

Initial demands for hostages are extreme. Experienced negotiators know that most hostage takers are more flexible than they first appear. The agent for Alex Rodriguez reportedly told the Yankees they'd have to pay $350 million just to enter into negotiations. The Yankees called the bluff and declined.

You can't bluff a bad product onto the market for long, but you certainly can when you negotiate. As Powell elegantly puts it, "You don't know what you can get away with until you try."

Guy Laliberte, founder of Cirque du Soleil, who finished fourth in a WPT championship and won almost $700,000, pulled off a great business bluff. His idea was still in its infancy, and he couldn't even get his tents up. Ignoring the reality, through the sheer force of his personality, he pitched his idea to the Quebec government, which bought it.

In 1975, Gates made a call to the company that was making the world's first personal computer. "I offered to sell them software. I worried they would realize I was just a student in a dorm and they'd hang up on me. Instead they said, 'We're not quite ready. Come see us in a month,' which was a good thing because we hadn't written the software yet."

I had given some of my time to develop an educational business. I contributed some material, and in return I was to receive a monthly income, but the owner was under no obligation to use my content. After the business was up and successful, the owner decided to make a lowball offer to buy out all of my material, with the threat that if I didn't accept he'd dump my content. I spent 10 minutes with my attorney, and he advised me I had no legal position (no cards). I decided on two strategies: a cold stone bluff and wear him down. I pretended to be insulted by his offer (act strong when weak, as Caro says). I told him I'd settle for 75 times what he'd offered me (an over-bet). After extensive correspondence back and forth for several months (wear him down) and the continuous, implied threat of a lawsuit (bluff with second and third barrel), I was able to negotiate an amount 10 times more than the original offer. Any great poker player would have known immediately what I was doing.

Bluff outs are used only when you really know your opponent and how he plays. They are the scare cards that can appear on the turn or river, usually the river, that will scare your opponent into folding the best hand if you bet. Without going into an extensive discussion, by the time you count your real outs and add in the bluff outs, you could be talking about over half the deck.

Dead money is what folders have put into the pot or what is available for you to steal with a big bet. Negreanu says about no-limit tournaments, "When you strip the game of poker down to the core, it is a battle for the blinds and antes. The blinds and antes dictate how many hands you should play and even if you should invest in a hand." To that I'll add a recent innovation: bounties on certain players. Most of the blinds and antes are dead money, and the more dead money in the pot, the more the payoff (pot odds) is increased, the more great players aggressively go after it.

Dead money in business occurs during product infancy and growth, when several competitors that enter the market help to build up customer acceptance and then, for one reason or another, abandon the market. The more dead money from your competitors, the more the market has been developed, the greater your payoff if you can capture a significant market share. Anytime you find several competitors who have invested substantial time, marketing, and other resources to develop a market, the result is a lot of dead money for the market leader. When Denali abandoned its bid to build natural gas pipelines in Alaska, it left the door wide open for its only competitor, TransCanada, to capture the entire market.

If you are the market leader, it's the investment competitors have put into building up the market that essentially creates customers for you. Then, for whatever reason, a competitor leaves the market. Its time and investment fill the market (the pot) with dead money. It's basically free money for you if you can capture market share.

Every once in a while you'll have a hand so good from start to finish that all you have to do is figure out how much to extract from your opponents. You have a high pair, and you flop a boat — AK suited and flop the nut flush. It happens in business too. Think of Hulu, the Apple iPhone, and Facebook. Within your lifetime, those who have access to clean water will have a hand that plays itself.

Outcomes and payoffs are not the same. The outcome of a hand is if you won or lost. The dollar payoff is how much you won or lost. Although dollar payoffs are easy to quantify, there are psychological payoffs that are much more difficult to measure.

In poker, you want to change your opponent's payoffs so that you put his mind in a place that works best for you. It might be changing his dollar payoffs by always raising and reraising or never folding to his raise. Perhaps it's showing him a bluff.

I can choose to play online or go to the casino. I know I can make more playing online by multi-tabling and playing many more hands. But let's suppose I know a friend is playing at the casino and I really enjoy his company. My dollar payoff is best online, but my psychological payoff is best at the casino.

We can also change our own payoffs. Young attractive women often hang out at certain clubs in the Hamptons or other target-rich areas because the potential payoff of a husband with a ton of money is much higher.

In a previous section, we talked about the game theory matrix for Bonnie and Clyde. The math analysis shown only goes so far. What happens if Bonnie really loves Clyde and knows that his mother has cancer and will die within the next year? Now you can see how the dynamics of the psychological payoffs (or the term "utility" in economics) for both prisoners change as Bonnie is more likely to do what she thinks is best for Clyde.

Everyone knows a parent can change a child's behavioral payoffs. Some of them are equivalent to dollar payoffs: that is, a specific reward or punishment. But the psychological impact of "I'm proud of you" or "I'm disappointed" often has much more force.

In the United States, we often hear that "the punishment should fit the crime." When I went to Virginia Tech, its code of honor (since abandoned) was strict: "I will not lie, cheat or steal or condone those that do." Here's an example of how enforcement changed the payoffs for offenders.

One night I was awakened at 2 a.m. The upperclassmen told us to get into uniform. None of the normal commands was given as we marched to a secluded part of the campus. The only sound was the taps as they clicked on the pavement. It was so dark I couldn't even see my classmate marching directly in front of me.

Two miles later, I started to hear a drum. Thu . . . thump! Thu . . . thump! As we got closer to the sound, I saw a light — two large burning torches. Each torch was about 10 feet high. I saw someone standing between the two fires. As I looked out of the corner of my eye, I could see the entire corps being assembled. Several thousand of us.

The drum stopped. Surrounding the torches on all sides were the corps, all directly facing the person standing alone. It was as quiet as an empty church. A loud voice bellowed out the charges. The cadet in the middle had been found guilty of stealing. He was told he was banished forever from Virginia Tech. I don't recall the words, but my 16-year-old heart was pounding. In a few minutes, it was over. The cadet was stripped of his uniform, honor, and dignity. On one command, everyone did an about-face and marched away from the thief.

Here's another example of changing payoffs. Notice how proportionality doesn't apply. When the world was ruled by Rome, no one dared touch a Roman citizen. If you did, a Roman army would come to your village, impale you and your family and another 1,000 in the village, and leave all the bodies on the spears until they rotted off. That's changing payoffs.

Roman soldiers wouldn't tie up their prisoners overnight. They'd draw a line in the sand and instruct the prisoners to be there the next morning. Anyone not on the line at first light was hunted down and executed. That's where the term "deadline" comes from.

How does our government change business payoffs? One way is through taxes. All politicians know, or should know, they change business payoffs by using the 70,000+ pages of our tax code. They get more of what they want via tax credits and less of what they want via direct taxation. Some politicians don't understand how they are changing pay-offs and don't understand they get less of something when they tax it or get more unemployment when they pay for unemployment. Another way they change payoffs is with laws and their enforcement. As I was writing this book, a local man was convicted of first-degree sexual assault of a 10-year-old disabled girl. The punishment? Judge Elliott Levine of La Crosse, Wisconsin, gave him probation. Not a single day in jail. A few weeks later, he gave probation to another rapist. Then a local judge, Scott Horne, awarded probation to yet another sexual offender. Time served and electronic bracelets, but no real punishment. Virginia may be for lovers, but Wisconsin is for rapists.

Nesson was the behind-the-scenes strategic thinker in the following case. A young man had copied some tunes and let several others on the Internet have access to them. The music industry sued. Nesson could have called, stating his client didn't do it. The way you change your opponent's poker payoffs is to raise. Nesson raised by saying that, even if his client did it, it was protected under the First Amendment as free speech. Look how his raise changed the potential payoff to the music industry. If the court ruled Nesson's argument correct, then anyone could destroy the industry.

Changing psychological payoffs isn't easy. In fact, it's one of the most difficult things we can ever attempt to do. But just because it's difficult doesn't mean we avoid it. It means we have to know our stakeholders well and figure out how to get their minds in a place that works best for all.

During a critical part of my first experience in court, the judge told the jury to leave the room and then told me I should settle the case. I turned to my attorney and said, "I haven't done anything wrong." My attorney said, "Right and wrong have nothing to do with what goes on in here." (Over the years, I have found his comment to be right; judges are more interested in shutting down cases and moving the docket along than searching for truth and justice.) I decided not to fold. The jury awarded me a six-figure judgment. During depositions, I'd found out how wealthy my opponent was. I made him an offer in which we could both come out ahead. I'd pass on the judgment if he'd guarantee a loan of several million dollars so I could expand my business. He accepted. A good deal for both of us.

If up against an adversarial competitor, try to get his mind in a place that works best for you. What is best for him? What is worst for him?

The best result is when everyone's payoffs are changed for the better, such as when Cisco and Microsoft collaborated to achieve customer satisfaction by creating solutions for those who wanted to mix and match products and technologies from both companies. John Chambers, CEO of Cisco: "If you do what is right for the customer, the whole industry will grow. Even though we might each have a smaller share in the market, there will be a much bigger pie for everyone. And we'll all make a lot more money" (Reardon).

When I say resources for business, I don't just mean money. Included are time and talent. Tournament play teaches you how to manage limited resources, your chip stack, a skill everyone in business needs. Seldom are resources symmetrical. After a few tournament hands, the chip stacks change. *We* use drones, *they* can't. For a publicly held company, this is information available to all.

Your chip stack is all about effective resource management. When you are the chip leader in a tournament, one effective strategy is to take charge of the table. You can afford to take a loss. In business, if you have the most resources, you can create high barriers to entry or make it too expensive for competitors to stay in the market. Monsanto genetically modified soy seed, then employed high-priced lawyers to create a patent that kept competition out.

In a tournament, as a pro's stack starts to dwindle, the pro limps with any kind of drawing hand. His objective is to get to the flop on the cheap. As his stack becomes smaller, he knows he can't wait for a premium hand, or he'll be blinded out. He must have enough chips with an all-in to make his opponents at least think about folding.

The strong animal can run for its life. You are Sun Tzu's wounded animal, who is more dangerous than a healthy one. When you are the first to act, you must gamble and go all-in with the most marginal of hands, even A-rag. You must double up to stay in the tournament. If possible, target an opponent who has a medium or short stack since the big stack can afford to take a hit.

When your business resources are low, you might as well go down swinging. You can't wait while overhead, taxes, and other expenses eat up everything. Find an opportunity, even if it's far less than perfect, and go all-in. If possible, target a competitor who doesn't have vast resources.

Martha Stewart was on the short stack with her conviction of insider trading, but with incredible chutzpah she promoted her domestic goodies from prison. Favre wouldn't let the clock beat him. He threw the risky pass because he wasn't interested in Tarkenton statistics; he was out to win. On 24 December 1776, George Washington was short stacked. Faced with desertions, low supplies, and a skeleton army, many of whom were sick, he decided to go all-in with a desperate attack the next day. He issued the password for that night: "Victory or death."

Against a lone short-stacked opponent who goes all-in, it doesn't matter how big your chip stack is. The most you can win are the chips he has put in. The effective stack is the amount of his bet, not what you have available.

Against a sole competitor who throws all of his money into a product, at least at that point in time, the market will be no greater than the sum of his and your investments. However, unlike poker, you can continue developing the market with more investment.

In class, we always emphasize limited resources, our effective stack. Students then ask me where I think resources should be committed. My response is always the same: "You cannot spend enough knowing your customers, your staff, and your competitors." A little overstated, but I think they get the point. I also emphasize that, if they don't know the answer to a marketing exam question, they should say something along the line of "understand your customers," and they'll probably get some credit for it.

Coastal Contacts, one of the largest online contact lens retailers in North America, came out of its two-day planning session at a loss for how to rev up growth. So, over the next six months, CEO Roger Hardy and his senior team called customers each week to see whether they had any ideas. To the company's surprise, one recurring theme emerged: customers wanted lenses the next day. "We started overnighting everything," he reported. U.S. sales increased over 40% in one year (Macht).

The chip leader has the high ground. Unless you know your hand is the best, you are better off picking a weaker target.

> *If the enemy occupies the high ground, do not confront him.* — *Sun Tzu*

The big stack in business is the one with the most resources and experience. If that's not you, unless your product is a star, avoid the big dog.

Deception without lying isn't cheating. Deception is always part of competition. Act as if you don't know when you really do know. Feign a move to see the reaction. Throw a teaser out of the strike zone.

> *Even though you are competent, appear to be incompetent.*
> *Though effective, appear to be ineffective.* — *Sun Tzu*

A mixed strategy keeps your opponents guessing. Random deception is always better. I use my hole cards to randomize my preflop play. If I want to do something 25% of the time, I use the suit of my right hand to tell me what to do. For example, I don't always want to raise with a high pocket pair, or everyone will know what I have. Let's suppose I decide I want to raise 75% of the time with a big pair. If my right-hand card is a Heart, I just call; otherwise, I raise. If I want to do something 50% of the time, I use the color of my right-hand hole card to tell me what to do. On the flop, I use the color or suit of the middle card.

If your opponent doesn't know what he's going to do, it's tough for you to figure out what he's going to do. If you don't know what you're going to do, it's tough for your opponent to figure out what you're going to do.

Many of the best players use a small-ball approach in deep-stack tournaments. The initial objective is to survive the early and middle stages. It requires a lot of experience and skill. Cut down to its basics, it's designed to keep ahead of the average tournament chip stack without assuming a lot of risk. It involves being in many hands on the cheap, seeing what develops on the board, then using postflop skills to outplay lesser opponents or folding if the betting gets too heavy. Tournaments are won in the trenches by aggressively going after little pots. The strategy includes avoiding playing big pots when the difficult decision is put to you and playing big pots when you think you have the best hand.

Small ball applied in business means that, as you become more experienced, more confident in your play, you'll bet on many more products without making huge investments. You want to get to the flop on the cheap and see how the market, your product, and your brand develop. Some don't believe in small ball. It's surprising to me that Boeing, a hugely successful company, makes an all-in bet with the B-787 Dreamliner. Small ball means avoiding all-in investments, and this is the way most operate. Small risks with marginal hands are better in the long run. Again, the tortoise and the hare.

The best hands (full houses, flushes, straights) can't be made until at least the flop but are seldom made on the flop. They are made on the turn or river. Until they are made, they usually start off as drawing hands. Such hands require an investment, usually a relatively small one, to see the flop. But drawing hands preflop almost always turn out to be either folding or still drawing hands on the flop. The turn is where the pot goes up geometrically and where we start talking about a major investment.

Great business products are usually the result of drawing hands. They didn't require much investment to do some initial research (to see the flop). But somewhere along the line, if the decision is made to go forward (to see the turn), a big investment (time, talent, or treasure) is required.

One drawing strategy is to compete against yourself by offering similar products with different brand names or another location within your trade area. Starbucks' purchase of Seattle's Best Coffee was definitely a drawing hand but turned out to be a brilliant winner by appealing to a different market, those who wouldn't be caught dead in a Starbucks (Henningfield).

Some hands take longer to develop than others. Going all the way to the river on a draw is expensive. But if the expected value (pot odds versus hand odds) is still positive, then you should continue in the hand. A smart opponent will see that you are on a draw and make a bet high enough so you don't have a positive EV (in poker language, "priced out"), forcing you to make the correct mathematical decision and fold.

Seeing a new product to the end will be expensive. If the payoff is high enough, and if the product is successful, you pay the price all the way to the river. If a competitor creates a barrier too high, unless the implied odds are there, the correct mathematical decision is to fold. Money saved is truly money earned.

And, as you look at more drawing hands, you'll also find that your most successful products only develop after you, and your competitors, have invested in the flop and possibly later.

If you never lay the best hand down, you call way too much. When the situation changes (the board), depending on your opponents, you have to know when to get out. The pro asks himself a minimum of two questions when considering a lay down. First, what are the pot odds (i.e., the return on investment)? Second, how often does this opponent bluff? If the pot odds are good, or he is up against someone who bluffs a lot, the pro usually calls. If the pot odds are poor, or he is up against a passive-tight, he folds.

If you never discard a product too early, you probably continue to throw good money after bad too often. When considering dropping a product, use the poker pro's method. What is the return on investment? Not the past investment, the future investment. Likewise, if we are up against a competitor who continues only with strong products, we should consider folding.

Fred Smith, CEO of Federal Express, was a pioneer of the fax machine. With mounting costs and uncertain market acceptance, he decided to fold. He didn't know it, but he was within an inch of the goal line. Competitors waiting in the wings took the fax machine and made it a winner.

If you have isolated an opponent with aggressive betting preflop, and you are first to act on the flop, you should almost always bet again, regardless of what appears on the board. A continuation bet of half the pot has to win just a third of the time for you to break even, but a heads-up continuation bet takes down the pot over 40% of the time — a good deal. That's because, unless your opponent is paired preflop, his chances of catching a pair on the flop are only one in three. The continuation bet should be used less frequently against an aggressive-loose who likes to three-bet (i.e., reraises your raise).

If there are two opponents to see the flop, the math changes, but if both opponents are tight a continuation bet is worth a stab. When you have three or more opponents on the flop, unless you actually have a hand, forget the continuation bet.

If you were first to market against just one major competitor, throw in another investment to try to get him to abort the mission. If you have several competitors, unless you actually have a good to superior product, the general rule is to fold.

Once you put money into the pot, it doesn't belong to you anymore. It's essentially your dead money. It belongs to the pot and whoever eventually wins the pot. How much you have already put into the pot has no effect on your decision to stay in, or at least it shouldn't.

It's like standing in the checkout line. Even though one of the lines starts to move faster, watch how many people will stay in their own, slowly moving lines. They think they have too much time invested in their lines to move. We should never use past sunk costs as an excuse to keep pouring money in.

Jon Friedberg, WSOP bracelet winner and CEO of Reactrix Systems, says, "You might have $10,000 invested in a hand, but once the turn card comes out everything changes, and the whole landscape of that hand is now completely different. It takes a lot of discipline to walk away from certain hands with money invested, just as it does for businesses to walk away from certain investments."

Correct business and poker decisions are made on potential gain versus potential loss at the moment, not on how much has been invested in plant and equipment or in the pot. We never throw good money after bad.

Great players don't pay opponents off when they know they can't win. When their top two pair meet the flush or straight draw on the river, and those still in the hand are betting and raising, the pros know to fold. Traders know they should cut their losses no matter how much they have already invested. We must do the same with our products.

You will make your flush only slightly more than five percent of the time. And you will win with your flush only three percent of the time. You will lose to a boat (that's why I slow down when the board pairs) or a better flush. If you have a Jack high flush with no higher flush card on the board, if someone else also has a flush, you'll win only 50% of the time. And a flush on the board is so obvious that seldom will you get paid off big time.

Marginal products are equivalent to second-best flushes. They might be necessary to fill out a product line or make a small contribution to overhead, but as stand-alone investments they seldom produce substantial returns. Even if the market accepts the product, the payoffs are often insignificant.

Marginal products are also comparable to marginal starting hands. You might get lucky and get bottom two pair on the flop, but by the river you'll often be counterfeited.

Hasbro's G.I. Joe nurse doll was a colossal flop. Boys didn't want to play with a girl doll, and girls didn't want anything to do with G.I. Joe. Anheuser-Busch developed, introduced, and marketed a low-priced marginal product, Natural Pilsner, even though I'm sure the company realized it would never have outstanding sales or profits (Rosenblatt).

As the poker student becomes more experienced, he widens the range of hands he plays. Intentionally, his play becomes looser. Whether in business or poker, the better player you are, the more flops you should see. Eventually, the student moves into higher-stakes games and plays a wide range of hands, even out of position.

Microsoft isn't afraid to try loose products. Some pan out, others don't.

Sometimes the situation demands taking an immediate risk. After an explosion on Apollo 13, the crew were forced to move from the command module into the lunar module, but it had too much carbon dioxide for the entire crew. The canisters for filters in the command module were square, and those in the lunar module were round. The astronauts would have died shortly if a risk wasn't taken. Using things here and there from the lunar module, clever engineers at mission control MacGyvered a filter that allowed the command module canisters to fit into the lunar module's filters (Nighbor).

Legal collusion. Often in a tournament, when a strong player is short stacked and goes all-in, the remaining players say nothing to each other but will call and check it down to the river. Why? It's to the advantage of all players to eliminate the top player, and they know if they all stay in the hand all the way to the river they have a great chance of eliminating that player.

Don't believe it? Let's suppose you know the top player has AA when he goes all-in at a 10-handed table. As stated previously, if everyone plays to the river, he has only a 30% chance of winning; better said, the players have a 70% chance of knocking him out if they do nothing but check it down all the way to the river. And the chances of him having AA are less than half of one percent in the first place, meaning that, if you don't know what he holds, the probability of knocking him out is well over 70%. Recall that even 72 will beat AK a third of the time (actually 32.8% with a 0.4 tie with rainbow suits).

Unlike the United States, in some countries it is perfectly acceptable for competitors to collude. Dividing up markets, controlling pricing, you take this product, and I'll take that. Those who don't collude take an unnecessary risk. BMW and Peugeot collaborated in an attempt to create a standard for hybrid and electric car technology. Their standard, if accepted by competitors, will allow both to share in an increasing market (Hanson).

But what can you do legally in the United States? If prevented by antitrust or some other regulation, we can send smoke signals to each other. Let's raise our price and see what everyone else does. Let's start charging for airline bags and see if our competitors follow.

How about illegal collusion? Cheating. There are players today who will signal to their teammates which cards they hold or have folded. Others mark certain cards. There are CEOs who don't hesitate to price fix with a competitor. Robert Crandall, American Airlines CEO, called the CEO of Braniff and said, "Raise your g------ fares 20%. I'll raise mine the next morning. You'll make more money, and I will too" (Melby).

Often the best business approach is when we can legally and morally cooperate with competitors and all end up with a slice of a much larger pie. The rising tide lifts everyone's boat.

Although its practice would be illegal in the United States, we know OPEC collaborates on price. It tries to find that point of maximum revenue where the price it charges doesn't cause an offsetting reduction in demand. After it attempts to maximize the pie, it fights for market share and worries about the size of its slice (Rosenblatt).

A food drive was being held in Portland, with drop boxes to be located at various businesses. To increase customer traffic, businesses naturally preferred to have the drop boxes only on their sites but dropped their competitive stances for the good of the drive (Henningfield).

> *Just as I change strategies as the conditions of the poker table change, I change my business tactics as the market changes. — Jeff Amrein*

The dynamics change with new players at the table or during different stages of a tournament. The great players adapt and change their play based on the situation. We've talked about playing differently than the table and the importance of knowing each opponent's playing style, chip stack, and myriad other factors. But we haven't yet talked about the different strategies used in various stages of a tournament. Let's examine how they vary depending on how deeply stacked the tournament starts off and how quickly the blinds and antes increase.

Deep-starting stack, blinds increase slowly.

- *Early stage.* When out of position, most pros play aggressive-tight; when in position, they play fairly aggressive-loose. They go for small pot steals when in position and avoid large pots unless they have strong hands. A big advantage in this early stage strategy is that opponents will see you go for steals, and when you actually have a hand you'll get paid off.
- *Middle stage.* The pro shifts toward aggressive-loose while avoiding big pots and difficult decisions.
- *End stage.* Now, when blinds and antes are high in relation to the average chip stack, most of the best players are in full aggressive-loose mode.

Medium- to low-starting stack, blinds increase fast.

- Whenever you have a tournament in which the stacks are not deep and the blinds increase quickly, there's a lot more gambling required. Translation: aggressive-loose from the start. There will be a lot of shoving going on.

At the start, you can foresee that some products will cost a lot to bring to market and that some won't. Similar to a medium stack going up against the chip leaders, if a company has many financially strong competitors, it understands that to compete it will require substantial future investments. There's little likelihood of knocking out those competitors at the start.

When Jeff Smisek took over the merged Continental and United Airlines, he held back on copying the trend of competitors of increasing capacity by adding more and more seats. Rather, he took the approach of seeing how much demand existed before making a decision (Jansen).

New poker players hate it when they ask me a question and I reply, "It depends." It really does depend on a whole bunch of variables. There are few real absolutes in poker, business, or life. The words *never* and *always* apply only to ethics.

I have often stated poker or business "rules" are something to follow. Are they good or bad? Neither. Nothing can be taken as unconditional. They are situational guidelines on which to base your decisions. You must consider a rule as it relates to the circumstances. There is no ultimate truth.

The moves are the tactics of any game. And they vary according to the player's view of the situation and his style. We can find victory among players and CEOs who have a style of play completely different from that of other successful leaders.

> *There are no right answers at the poker table and no right style.*
> *I am a firm believer in the adage that there are as many ways to win*
> *at poker as there are poker players. — Howard Lederer*

Ask More Questions, Get More Answers

One of the Click and Clack brothers (I think it's the one who snorts when he laughs) constantly asks the caller questions. When a doctor doesn't know what's going on, he asks more questions. You must be the doctor. With open-ended questions, you tend to get a mixture of information and opinion. With a closed, yes-or-no question, usually you get just an opinion.

In a tournament, you can't choose your opponents or the table you play, but in a cash game you can. Unless I'm trying to test myself, I never sit at a table with those better than I am. If several pros sat down at my table, I'd leave. This is an important concept. You should seldom wander into an industry in which you are up against superior dogs. If a Walmart opens next to your grocery store, move. As well, you should never enter a market that will turn out to be too small.

An expert in Texas Hold'em will lose a lot when he first starts playing Omaha unless he goes through the same learning experiences he went through to become great at Hold'em. He must use two of his four cards, understand who is betting on the high and who is betting on the low. Every new game requires new areas of expertise.

> *From poker, I learned the most important decision I could make was which table to sit at. In business, one of the most important decisions for an entrepreneur or CEO to make is what business to be in. It doesn't matter how flawlessly a business is executed if it's the wrong business or if it's in too small a market. In a poker room, I could only choose which table I wanted to sit at. But in business, I realized that I didn't have to sit at an existing table. I could define my own or make the one that I was already at even bigger. — Tony Hsieh*

I once told Augie Nieto, CEO of Life Fitness, I had a vision of someone walking into a health club and, as he walked in, a scanner would automatically check him in, tell him his weight, body mass index, history of workouts, other physical indicators, and then prescribe a personalized workout for the day. When I asked him to create this new product, he smartly said, "I stick to my knitting. I know how to create the best computerized workout equipment in the world, and that's what we'll do."

Play the game in which you know which questions to ask. Play the game you understand.

If an inexperienced player has any chance against the pros in a tournament, he needs to have a shove (at least a pot bet) or fold mentality. He waits for premium hands. He tries to get the hand over preflop or on the flop and never let it get to the turn, as that's where the pros will outplay him. The pots he wins are small, as he seldom has many callers. This type of play takes away the skill of the better player, who is forced to sit around and wait for a premium hand.

The all-in tactic works every time. Until it doesn't. Ted Turner parlayed one successful venture into another and doubled down again, becoming the largest shareholder of Time Warner. He lost $7 billion when Time Warner's stock collapsed. By the way, notice that the chip leader on day one of the tournament, the one who is going all-in, is usually gone by the third day.

If you are relatively new in business, a similar strategy is to invest heavily, essentially a shove or pot bet, in one or two great products, hoping your competitors will get out of the way. This is an approach used by many successful entrepreneurs since they are betting on potential star products.

With several competitors, we keep the pressure on with a good product. But against strong competitors, when our business life is on the line, requiring an all-in investment, why risk everything? If we are the superior businessperson, and trust that in the long run our decisions will be better, there is no reason to risk it all.

Another approach is the one in *Built to Last*, using what the company stands for as the anchor rather than relying on a product. This tends to work best when you clearly understand your core values and are fortunate enough to hit a product early in the life of the business.

Even if you fail, just wait for the next hand to be dealt. Edison failed thousands of times before he invented the lightbulb.

Many professionals will play opposite to the rest of the table. If the table is loose, they play tight; if the table is tight, they play loose.

During economic downturns, Cisco's competitors hunkered down in Asian markets while Cisco increased its hiring and marketing efforts with excellent results.

When other energy firms backed off in Brazil due to the extreme devaluation of its currency, an Italian firm, Eni, invested heavily. It entered the market betting on a turnaround of the Brazilian economy. Today Brazil has recovered, and Eni is a market leader (Rosenblatt).

During a recent recession, many online sales companies focused on cost reduction by offshoring customer service. Zappos took a completely different route. Its call representatives focused on understanding the needs of customers as opposed to order taking and quick turnover of calls. Zappos also went against the tide with both free shipping and free return shipping (Rosenblatt).

Marc Beinoff created Salesforce.com because he started questioning the status quo of loading and upgrading software. His concept was to play opposite to the rest of the table by providing software via the Internet. Now the rest of the table is copying him (Fritz).

Another strategy is to differentiate. Eddie Bauer distinguished itself from all competition with one of the first unconditional guarantees: "Every item we sell will give you complete satisfaction, or you may return it for a full refund." Unconditional means unconditional. It doesn't matter if you bought it 10 years ago and don't have a receipt.

Haidilao, a Chinese hot pot restaurant, not only offers delivery but also a personal waiter. When the delivery person comes, he brings the food, a hot pot, a portable electric hot plate, and aprons for the customers. He sets the table and comes back when they are finished to pick up the hot pot, hot plate, and even the trash (Fritz).

Sherlock Holmes: "Once you eliminate the impossible, whatever remains, no matter how improbable, must be the truth." Once we know what can't occur, we can eliminate it. Holmes identified the killer as one who was known to the dog. Because the dog didn't bark.

There are always variables that can be disregarded. If I have the Ace of Spades, three Spades appear on the flop, and an opponent makes a big bet, what do I know? I know he can't have the nut flush. If he is a top pro who uses the small ball approach during the early and middle stages of a tournament, I will go all-in since he'll probably not risk his tournament life on the possibility that I have the nut flush. Even if he calls, I can still catch.

How did scientists conclude that humans were using tools over 3 million years ago? They looked at the bones of prehistoric animals. They saw no teeth marks, which meant animals hadn't torn the meat off. There was no post-fossilization damage. There were no breaking points on the smaller bones, and all breaking points on the larger bones were uniform, ruling out trampling by other animals. The bones had several clear, straight marks. And carbon dating showed them to be over 3 million years old. Once they had eliminated the impossible, the only conclusion possible was that the marks had been made by humans using spears (Prasad).

Some players relish the final table; others tighten up. There's always someone in your organization who wants the responsibility, while others are more cautious.

I tell my students that, if they want to get promoted fast, become known as the one who wants the ball. Here are the only words I recommend ever coming out of their mouths: "Yes," "No," "No excuse," "I'll take care of it."

If both answers to a "yes" and "no" question are alarming, you don't have the answer yet.

Do I call? The math player believes he's beat but sees the inviting pot odds and figures he doesn't have to call this river bet often to be profitable.

Shelton, with a life-threatening wound in Vietnam, "Do I tell my wife?"

The boyfriend who first asks "Are you pregnant?" and then asks "Is the baby mine?"

When Gates was still a student at Harvard and asked the computer manufacturer if it wanted his operating program (and he hadn't even written it yet).

Do we issue the recall?

Jim is the last one hired but has turned out to be a great employee. We are faced with downsizing. Do we fire him?

Should you bring in outside investors into your business?

You are the CEO of a very successful company. You have just received an internal confidential report of a soon-to-be-implemented new government regulation that will cause both your profits and your sales to plummet. A good friend asks if he should invest in your company.

What will give you your greatest opportunity if you can only make it happen? We don't wait for the right conditions. We make the conditions right.

IBM sees great opportunities with a "smarter planet" philosophy. It attempts to "make it happen" by investing in esoteric advances in artificial intelligence (Watson), automated medicine, and cloud computing (Reineke).

My first business venture, indoor tennis courts, required a staggering amount of money, and I had only $600 to my name. So I created a limited partnership, literally started knocking on accredited investors' doors, and eventually raised what was needed.

Are you looking through the right end of the telescope? This is an oft-repeated theme. Are we looking at everything not just through our own perspectives but also understanding the perceptions of our stakeholders and competitors? Consider the businessperson who won't legally cooperate with a competitor even though it might result in a bigger pie. Or the stockbroker who focuses on the sale of a stock as opposed to whether it's right for his client. Or the overburdened judge who looks for ways to dismiss the case. Or caring about how much profit the seller is making as opposed to the benefits you are receiving with the purchase. Or the businessman who closes the deal instead of going to his daughter's graduation.

If you can figure out why something is happening, your move often becomes obvious. This is the key to Nesson's riddle. Becky was aware of what was going on around her. She noticed that neither Sarah nor Ashley, both highly intelligent women, could solve the puzzle. Therefore, Becky realized she must have a red hat on.

If there is correlation, is there true causation? Just because A precedes B doesn't mean A caused B.

On Sundays, I often play poker on a Mississippi riverboat. Several think a specific seat is lucky since they have seen a player get good cards often. It's not the seat, it's the meat in the seat (Seif).

Doctors seek information to try to find out what is causing the symptoms. Business leaders dig for knowledge to understand their customers, competitors, and staff. Such understanding usually provides the answer to "Why is this happening?"

Momentum has nothing to do with math but everything to do with psychology. Who has the momentum? A player who is winning has more confidence, and the table reacts to it. When a player has been catching cards, others begin to fear him.

A classic rookie mistake in both poker and business is quitting when ahead. If you are going to abandon a product, do so when you are losing, not when you are winning. In the stock market, business, and poker, cut your losses short and let your profits ride.

Anyone can feel the energy, or lack of it, in an organization. We lead by example — for better or worse. It sets the tone.

> *Launch, keep moving, keep learning, keep getting experience.* — Brian Tracy

Caesar wore a red cape into battle. He told his troops he wanted to give the enemy a target, but he was really letting them know he was willing to do anything he asked of them by leading from the front. McAllister: "'Follow me' vs. 'Take the hill. I'll watch from the rear.'" Shelton: "I enjoy sharing in the dangers that we ask our men and women in uniform to share almost every day."

A few good results and the leader becomes more positive. You can see

> *Perpetual optimism is a force multiplier.*
>
> — *Colin Powell*

it in his eyes. That confidence flows to everyone in the organization. It makes others feel upbeat. The hearts of others are engaged. It becomes an upward spiral of personal momentum. The company makes leaps. It's Sun Tzu's "combined energy."

> *There's no limit to how much you'll know,*
>
> *depending on how far past zebra you go.* — *Dr. Seuss*

There is no substitute for accurate, relevant knowledge. Never stop asking questions. The more answers you have, the more self-confident you are. As you become more self-confident, everyone around you does too.

This was a very long chapter. I hope you noticed that the bulk of it dealt with people. All great leaders, all great poker players know that at least 80% of life and success is people, and at most 20% is substance.

4

Negotiation

....

Bet, raise, offer, counteroffer. Every hand of poker is a negotiation. In business, you negotiate every day, sometimes as the buyer, sometimes as the seller. Negotiation is heads-up play. Mano y mano. One on one. Many view it as roadrunner versus coyote. Spy versus spy.

Negotiation as presented here is more Wei-Ch'i (it can also be spelled Wei Qi) than chess. Wei-Ch'i is an ancient Chinese game based on surrounding the other party. It's based on a slow, methodical, incremental strategy, and when the game is finished the uninitiated who looks at the board often can't tell who won. Chess is based on destroying the other party. Anyone who looks at the board can tell who won. You'll see that my approach is always the softer Wei-Ch'i first, then, if that hasn't worked, chess.

So far we have discussed snippets of negotiation. And at least half of this book relates to negotiation, but I realize it's better to repeat and expand a few things that will help you in every negotiation. Here's my personal checklist.

1. Write out what you want to accomplish, a specific goal. Of course, once you enter into the negotiation, your goal might change; if so, rewrite it. Refer to your goal often. Everything you do when negotiating should take you one step closer to your goal.

2. Prepare, prepare, prepare. You shouldn't view the other person as a competitor, but you must know everything about him, as discussed previously. We've discussed how the best players don't play a particular style but adjust their play according to their competitors, wanting to see things through their eyes. They play the player and the situation. The same applies in negotiation. Even though you might have had the same cards in the past, faced the same problem before, the solution should be found depending on the other person and the situation.

> *When you are in a poker hand, you have incomplete information, you are negotiating with people, there is an element of luck, there are probabilities that if you do your homework you can be better at predicting those probabilities than your opponent. It's a lot like life and relationships. — Ron Rubens*

Online players aren't nearly as good as live players in negotiation since live players have developed much better people-reading skills. Live players rely on physical tells at the poker table. Pupil dilation, blink rate, pursed or disappearing lips, pacifier behavior, gravity-defying behavior, position of palms, thumbs, movement toward or away from the table, voice inflection, all signify whether an opponent is comfortable or uncomfortable with his hand and situation (Navarro). Buffett: "If you've been playing poker for half an hour and you still don't know who the patsy is, you're the patsy." There's no difference during a negotiation. The signs are there if you know how to read them.

> *Acting persuasively, reading opponents' motives, and handling the subtleties of a monetary transaction are skills the poker greats work tirelessly to hone. These skills are essential for negotiating a business deal.*
> — *Douglas MacMillan*

If I know the other person before I sit at the table, I know whether I'm dealing with a person of honor and fairness or one who wants to squeeze everything for his benefit. It's then easier to look at everything from his point of view.

Before the negotiation starts, simulate role reversal in which someone who knows you plays you and you play the person you'll

> *Before entering the room, the best negotiators have taken both sides into account.*
> — *Donald Trump*

be negotiating with. This might sound hokey, but it's a worthwhile exercise since it gets you to think from his point of view and anticipate things that will probably be brought up.

3. Create an environment conducive to agreement. Make it comfortable for your counterpart. Understated, not formal, furniture. Less mahogany. Soft lighting. If there is a potential legitimate connection, include it. Let's say you know he skis with his family and you ski with yours. Include a picture of you and your family skiing. If he is a baseball fan, bring out that signed Mantle ball and place it on a side desk. I prefer a small circular glass table so I can interpret his full body language. At a minimum, you and he should sit on the same side of a rectangular table.

4. Ensure up front that you are dealing with the person who has the power to make a decision. "If we come to an agreement, do you have the power to commit to it?"

5. Your greatest assets in every negotiation are trust and credibility. Duplicity, half-truths, misinformation won't help you. If asked a direct question about something you don't want to divulge, a truthful "I'm not ready to discuss that right now" will suffice.

Remember that careful listening builds trust. It also allows you to gain information. You can find out where the other person falls in the Myers-Briggs. You can learn which words he uses. You can ask non-threatening but probing questions. You can gradually frame your own points just by the questions you ask. You can find out what he considers important and unimportant. Arimond: "In negotiating, there are always some points and issues that are more important than others. You need to figure out what is most important to others and touch on that message." You can break up the big problems into smaller ones. When each has a good feeling about the other, a fair solution becomes possible.

6. Go in with and maintain a passive, persistent, positive, patient, polite, calm, steady, transparent, constructive, soft, collaborative attitude. Negotiations should be approached in a graduated manner similar to how you'd approach a deep-stack tournament in which blinds increase slowly. In the early stages of those tournaments, our play is in the aggressive-tight quadrant of the passive aggressive tight loose (PATL) matrix (see Figure 3.5, page 98). As the tournament progresses, the best players move to the right in the matrix with aggressive-loose play. In negotiations, we move up the matrix, starting with passive play and moving, if necessary in later stages, to more aggressive play.

Initial passive play doesn't mean you don't have a hard outcome and firm payoff in mind, but there is no reason to go directly there. In many situations, if you follow everything on my checklist, you won't have to move past passive play.

This approach is easily taken when negotiating with customers, employees, or other stakeholders, but it works just as well with someone you might view as an opponent. Why is this passive first approach recommended? It builds a non-adversarial relationship. You'd prefer to do business with someone you like and trust. That's the way negotiations should start. The law of reciprocity applies. If you project harmony, most people will respond in kind. If you are collaborative, they will be too. The more positive the emotions, the more likely a positive outcome. There's another reason to start off passively: the negotiation will take more time. The shorter the time devoted to negotiation, the more adversarial it will be. The more time and effort invested, the more accommodation is reached.

7. Assume nothing. Make sure that both of you are using the same definitions of the words you are using and that there's agreement even on the obvious. "Just to make sure I understand, we both need to come to some agreement by Friday, correct?" Even if you've done extensive background research on the other person, use friendly questioning to ensure that you understand him, his feelings, his constraints, his thoughts, and what he is trying to accomplish. Agreements are 90% people, 10% substance (Diamond).

Calmly write down the things you both agree to. Even the smallest facts. Summarize often. Doing so accomplishes two things. First, you are showing agreement, and a small but important bond is developed. Second, your list will serve as a useful tool if the other person later forgets, intentionally or unintentionally, what has been agreed to. If you find yourself on the receiving end of a hard, manipulative negotiator more experienced than you, your position should shift: "Although I'm writing things down, let's agree that nothing is agreed to until everything is agreed to."

8. Take polite but persistent baby steps toward your goal. Every mini-agreement, even if it's just to take a break, is a step in the right direction since it builds collaboration. If you find you've made too great a leap for the other person to accept, back off a little. Two steps forward, one step back.

All great salespeople know that "No" doesn't mean "No." It's just a request for more information.

9. Make few statements, ask more questions (Diamond), float ideas without committing to them, and be empathetic.

- What are your goals?
- What are your needs?
- Tell me more.
- Would you consider . . . ?
- What if we . . . ?
- Suppose we . . . ?
- Please tell me where I'm wrong.
- I understand how you feel. If I was in your place, I'd probably feel the same way.
- I understand how you feel. Others have felt the same way, but they've found . . .
- I really need this, and here's why.

10. There are always concessions, sometimes major, often minor. Here the law of reciprocity, but not equal reciprocity, applies. If he makes what you consider to be a major concession, you should reciprocate with something that doesn't cost you much, if anything, but means something to him.

11. Write it up and sign it. As a graduate of the Air Force Academy, my employee wasn't part of a major cheating scandal. I trusted him. After a few years of working for me, he told me he had a personal crisis and needed a lot of money. I drained our savings and borrowed all I could and gave it to him. No promissory note. No documentation. He ran away with a woman, leaving his wife and children. He also ran away with all my money.

12. If you don't ask, you don't get.

Many of the passive principles of negotiation can and should be used in the group decision making discussed in the next chapter.

The best result of a negotiation is when the payoffs for both parties have been enhanced. If that's not possible, if you plan on ever working with the other person again, both of you should feel you worked hard and got something but also gave up something. Your price, my terms, or my price, your terms.

If I trust the other party, I don't mind putting the first proposal on the table, especially if I have superior information. Otherwise, I prefer to get the other side to lay out his proposal first. The power of position, you acting last, gives you control, just as it does in poker. When you have position, use it. When you don't, respect it.

In the discipline of accounting, where there are fewer PhD graduates, the tendency is for graduates to shop around, receive multiple offers, and then make their choices. In those instances, it's often better for the College of Business to be the last institution interviewed if we can determine not just the other offers but also the needs of the candidate and how we can satisfy those needs better than other institutions (May). Whoever has the most information, and that is almost always the person who has position, has the advantage.

If for some reason you must make your proposal first, one approach is to use the anchoring effect to your advantage. If you are willing to settle for $100,000, propose the highest amount you could possibly justify using the most optimistic assumptions. Let's say that is $150,000. The $150,000 will be an anchor for the other party. I've seen sophisticated, manipulative negotiators use the indirect anchor with "Did you see that piece of art sold for $150,000" and even the more oblique "The population of that city is about 150,000."

Sometimes a third-party expert can be used. "Since we're so far apart, let's get an appraisal." With a serious impasse, "Is there someone we both trust whom we could use to settle this?" Point out inconsistencies between what he has said in the past and what he is saying now.

When you are dealing with honorable people, the soft, passive approach almost always results in agreement. However, when dealing with those who refuse to be reasonable, you're in the middle stage of the negotiation tournament, and it's time to play more aggressively.

There are business wringers who try to get the hyphen in a 50-50 deal. Negreanu: "If I've made an offer, and I feel like I can get more on it, I'll continue to push until I feel the other guy is at his breaking point." That's not me. I'm in agreement with Berman, who learned this from his dad: "I don't buy at the absolute lowest price. I buy at a fair price. I have utilized this approach throughout my business career and never regretted it." Unless I'm up against a squeezer, I'm not the one who will try to wring the last quarter point; better that we both get a fair deal than I get the better deal. I'd prefer to build a long-term relationship as opposed to a one-time transaction.

My first business venture, indoor tennis courts, almost ended in disaster. I decided to have an audit done on my contractor since the project was a mere 30% over budget (and, of course, six months behind schedule). My only problem was I didn't have any money left. I went to the local partner of the Alexander Grant accounting firm and explained my situation, especially the part about my depleted bank account (actually a negative balance, but that's another story). He said, "We'll do the audit. Pay us when you can pay us." I told him I might never be able to pay him. He insisted he'd have the audit done. He saved me since the contractor was overbilling. He built a lifetime relationship. Over the years, I never even considered moving to another accounting firm, though I'd constantly get much lower bids from excellent firms.

If everything has failed, many turn to the aggressive late stage of the negotiation tournament with hard power bargaining. Anyone who chooses to use threats, intimidation, tension, and pressure should always employ them at the end, not at the start, of any negotiation.

If you are new to business litigation, here's a surprising stat.

Fewer than two percent of all lawsuits make it to trial.

Over 98% are settled. And many settlements occur on courthouse steps.

If you choose this path, realize that, once you go there, if it doesn't work, the chance to resume negotiation is gone. No long-term relationship is possible. As emotions become heated, rational thought is eliminated, and information cannot be processed. Those who employ these tactics know how to exploit the tipping points, hot buttons, and leaks of an opponent. They focus on changing his fear payoffs so drastically that he will have no choice but to capitulate.

5

Decision Making

Categorizing and Prioritizing Decisions

Which decisions are critical? Which aren't worth spending much time on? And which are in between? Which are permanent, and which can be reversed? Which are short term, and which are long term? See Figure 5.1 for the range of decision making.

Intuition is sufficient for everyday decisions. It's the ability to subconsciously take into account lessons learned, past patterns and analogies, your own life experiences and those of others, crisscrossing many different disciplines, filtering out what is unimportant, in an instant having an insight and making a decision. There's a good reason why the five year old has no intuition compared with the elder. The senior has the benefit of learned patterns and the ability to apply those patterns, while the novice does not.

> *Poker readily demonstrates that a person's actions do matter,*
>
> *that his decisions do have consequences. — Lyle Berman*

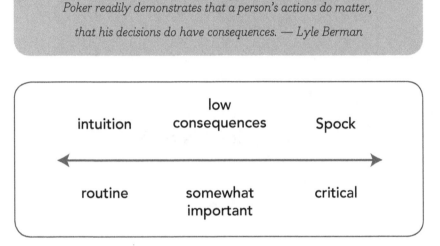

Figure 5.1 Range of Decision Making

You can develop usable mental maps fairly easily by using sight and sound. These associations are usually acceptable if not nearly good enough. Using your eyes and ears alone doesn't elicit many different pathways in the brain to recognize a relationship or analogy in hundreds of different ways.

Intuition is best among those who are accustomed to using all of their senses fully in innovative ways. They are lifelong learners, free from most biases, socially secure, and can recall the smallest details. They link a pattern strongly to an emotion. They are the few who use multiple pathways linking many parts of the brain, able to see relationships that others miss.

Chuck was often faced with a situation in which he had to guess where his opponent would hit the ball and move to that spot before the opponent made his shot. This is guess and go. It's based on probabilities. Chuck instantly had to take into account all of the information he had about his opponent, the stage of the match, the importance of the shot, and make a decision what to do, where to move.

We have discussed how poker players use intuition a lot. When logic says to do one thing, and intuition says to do another, almost all go with their hunches. In this regard, female players have an edge over male players. Women are much better at using all of their senses, relating their social and emotional experiences to the moment, and then using what they have learned about a particular opponent to see if the opponent's actions match or don't match previous associations and patterns.

When time permits, verify your hunch with more information. When both knowledge and experience coincide, the decision is easy. When you can't tell which outweighs which, the possession arrow points toward your instinct.

A good hockey player plays where the puck is. A great hockey player plays where the puck is going to be. — Wayne Gretzky

One hand usually doesn't hold many consequences unless you're in one of the $1 million Andy Beale heads-up pots or your tournament life is on the line. Most hands are of relatively low consequences.

A leader, especially during the introduction and growth phases, must make most decisions, tons of them, quickly with limited information. It's the learning period the online player goes through when he is multi-tabling too many turbo tables at once, making acceptable decisions but certainly not optimum ones. But since online play is more mathematical and less psychological, eventually just a good player will have a positive win rate.

McAllister: "I'm satisfied to get a high volume of decisions/actions with a trade-off of a 5–10% error rate. Sort of a 'decreasing marginal utility' on time invested." We will categorize these no-huddle plays as low-consequence or routine decisions.

Some decisions will have low consequences, or at least you think they will. They are important enough to spend some time on but not worth going through everything in the next section. For these decisions, I suggest this short version.

1. Define the problem.
2. Come up with solutions.
3. Run each solution through an ethics test.

4. Weigh pros and cons of each solution.
5. Choose a solution.
6. Choose a plan B.
7. Pull the trigger.

The Spock Decision-Making Model

When the needle rises to critical, you can't afford to depend solely on your natural thinking. Since poker is almost a one-person business, without a vast number of stakeholders, for the most part I will skip the poker analogies and move into a more complex decision world for business leaders.

Decisions are usually whether or which. Do we do it or not? Which do we choose? Critical decisions mostly fall under the whether category.

Buffett: "You're going to make mistakes in life. You don't want to make them on the big decisions, such as who you are going to marry." Big decisions should be made in a gradual, step-by-step, logical, analytical, unemotional, Spock-like process (recall that Spock was the non-emotional, purely logical Vulcan in the original *Star Trek* series).

We are not inherently the rational decision makers we think we are. Some "deciders" tend to act too fast. Failure to use a methodical approach when you're in the deep end of the pool leads to holes in any decision. The model I have found most effective when making a crucial decision is lengthy, as it should be. Tough choices demand meticulous rigor. Using this model will greatly reduce unforced errors. Most of these steps help to lower uncertainty and provide clarity, but at the end you'll see they also provide peace (Figure 5.2).

Although the steps are presented in a certain sequence, in practice you'll skip from one step to another, come back to a previous step, then leapfrog to still another. There's no straightforward way to make an important decision. Even so, make sure each step is complete. The more thorough you are, the wiser your decision. Although the model is designed to reduce decision-making traps, the perfect decision is impossible. There are few bright lines in poker, business, or life.

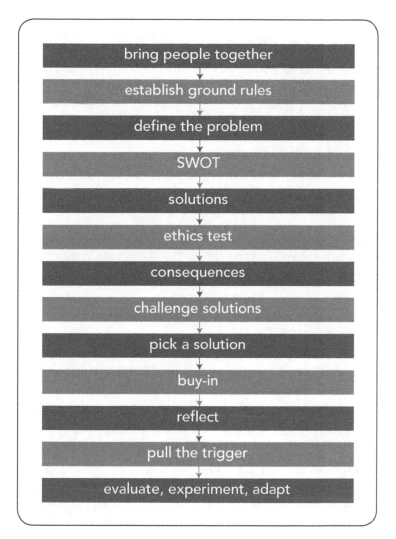

Figure 5.2 Decision-Making Model

To get the best use of the model we are about to explore, keep an open, curious mind, be ready to adjust as best you can for your prejudices and biases, gather information and turn it into knowledge, focus on the key knowledge points, and bounce things off the most-experienced and best minds available.

You'll also notice this expands the traditional "scientific method." It's also an advanced application of "critical thinking."

1. Define the problem.
2. Collect data.
3. Arrive at a hypothesis to solve the problem.
4. Test the hypothesis.
5. Draw a conclusion.

At the end of the chapter, I'll re-emphasize Powell's "All the great ideas and visions in the world are worthless if they can't be implemented rapidly and efficiently."

You'll see that this decision model is a group process. If you have already built a culture and similar company history that blends in with the ground rules and process, then you have a much higher probability of reaching a wise decision.

Bring People Together

Depending on the size of your organization, you might find you don't have the resources to do all that is recommended. I'll give you the "ideal," which you might have to modify.

"Not only do you want to come up with the wisest solution possible, but, at least as important, is to create a process that everyone will view as fair and legitimate" (Roberto), even if they don't agree with the final solution. There will be three teams. Each will have a different definition of the problem, and I'll explain those definitions in the next section. Three teams mean three of everything, except, of course, your management team, which will be split among the teams. Whom do you bring together?

A diversity of personalities, talents, departments, disciplines, and viewpoints is essential. A team with everyone who has similar personalities, backgrounds, or interests will seldom produce the best solutions.

Diversity of personalities and viewpoints isn't as easy to achieve as it first appears. Remember that your people, especially your management team, are a reflection of you — your personality and your viewpoint. More than likely, whether you think you do or not, you and your top managers have a very limited perspective. One way to broaden your viewpoint is by involving stakeholders up front. They usually have areas of informational expertise.

Identify your stakeholders and then divide them into primary and secondary groups. Among the primary groups, identify which of the following are most affected or have special knowledge of the situation.

- Family
- Customers, often broken down by segments
- Employees (not just executives) and their families
- Stockholders
- Board of directors
- Boss
- Lenders
- Vendors
- Community
- Government
- Environmental
- Social
- Political
- Religious

Competitors can be stakeholders if not adversarial.

Although it's always better to get everyone around the table, that's usually too cumbersome. In that case, get the opinion of each of your primary stakeholders who might be affected by the situation by holding focus groups and then have representatives of those stakeholders at the table.

They will usually include, at a minimum, customers and workers. Including a representative of those who might have to implement the solution is essential, not only because he will see obstacles and difficulties others don't, but also because you will need his buy-in to execute any solution. Once the process has started, often a team finds they later need to bring aboard representatives of different stakeholders or outside experts. They are free to do so.

Who else? Professional facilitators. One for each group. Although you might have on your management team some who are excellent facilitators, I recommend you bring in seasoned outsiders. It's just too much work for an insider to play the role of both a participant and a facilitator. Not only will the facilitators be involved in the all-day sessions, but they will also meet at the end of each day to share information as well as brief you each morning on the progress of each team. As new people are brought aboard, the facilitator must brief them and bring them up to speed.

Facilitators will also have to take on a number of other duties.

They have to keep things on track. This includes sharing information not just within their teams but also among teams (as part of their session reviews with other facilitators) and encouraging team members to leave the room and engage in conversations with individuals who might have specialized knowledge and then bring back what they have learned to the team.

They have to restate and clarify assumptions, ideas, or opinions. This involves testing to ensure that others understand by asking them to paraphrase another's point of view.

They need to identify and mitigate biases. This includes fostering vigorous but non-acrimonious debate.

They must keep the discussion flowing freely by drawing out areas the group is overlooking, searching for more options, asking more probing questions, not taking sides, ensuring that everyone has roughly the same time to speak, letting stakeholders argue it out but acting as peacemakers when debate becomes too emotional or personal, keeping the group listening carefully to all points of view and all information, and preventing the group from coming to a solution too quickly.

They should privately brief new people at the table and update others on the progress of each team.

Someone on each team (not the facilitator), or preferably two people, should play devil's advocate. When the pope needs to decide something important, he appoints both a devil's advocate and a God's advocate. One gives the reasons against and the other the reasons for. You don't need a God's advocate since almost all of your executives will endorse what they think you want.

Part of the devil's advocate's job is to fight groupthink, the natural tendency of individuals to conform to the majority. The devil's advocate should present contrary evidence and opinions and encourage and interject different thinking. He should be comfortable in, but not relish, this role. The best devil's advocate is one who knows how to ask discomforting questions without being intimidating. This involves a delicate personality dance since eventually there will be emotional friction as the debate rages on. He should criticize everything in all directions without ever cutting off any line of thinking. He is similar to the jester who constantly whispers into the king's ear, "All fame is fleeting." Roberto: "Effective devil's advocates are putting forth critiques in an attempt to ultimately strengthen a proposal or to open up a discussion by helping to generate lots of new options."

Include global, non-partisan thinkers. One for each group. Roberto: "To be a neutral, skeptical generalist." They are there to ask penetrating questions or come up with solutions the group is missing. Without them, you might just repeat history; with their advice, you might just make history.

If the situation involves an adversarial competitor, designate at least one person on each team to play the role of the competitor. His job is to interject what he would do to combat each potential solution. When poker players are preparing for a table with known opponents, other solid players will "role-play" the styles and betting patterns of opponents.

Someone who isn't really part of the team should act as a scribe. As a non-participant, he should record the process. Court reporters do a great job.

Diversity is important among teams. As the teams are formed, realize the most important balance is one of personalities and points of view, not of expertise or backgrounds.

Establish Ground Rules

You should establish ground rules that your facilitator is in charge of enforcing whenever you aren't in the room. Let team members know if you'll be in the room now and then or whether you prefer each team to come up with its own solution first. Depending on your style, if you are in the room, you'll be either an observer or an active questioner.

A retreat setting is best with only limited contact with corporate matters. Private or group conversations continue over meals and after set meeting times.

The playing field should be level. Everyone must check his ego, title, and position at the door. There is no protocol other than that everyone in the room is equal. That includes equal speaking time.

No one is to represent only his department or stakeholder interests.

Everyone is to act as someone trying to solve the problem regardless of his knowledge or expertise or lack of it. Everyone should be frank. Dissenting viewpoints are welcomed and expected. Everyone is to point out possible errors and risks even if those with more expertise disagree.

Let all teams know they will diverge and act independently for a while, each with a different definition of the problem, until they have arrived at a solution. No one from one team is to discuss anything with another team member until it's time to swap solutions. The teams will then converge and present their solutions to each other and, if they so wish, alter their solutions.

Teams are encouraged to bring aboard outside experts or representatives of other stakeholders. Anyone is allowed to gather independent information or speak with anyone outside his own team (except members of other teams).

Give all team members an outline of the decision-making process (Figure 5.2, page 183), and let them know they are welcome to depart from this roadmap if they so choose. Inform them if there is a time constraint. If not, they will meet all day until they have arrived at a solution. Even if there is not a deadline, mention that "There will come a time when debate must be cut off. I will give you ample warning before we get to that point." Tell them that "Regardless of your team's solution, I will then individually ask each of you the following: if you were me, what would you do and why? After everyone is heard, I will make my decision."

Now ground rules for yourself. Preferably, you have an open mind and are amenable to considering any solution. "We have a situation, and I need your help to decide what to do." However, if you already have a preference, don't attempt to hide that you do. Whatever you say and do must be in true character. The worst result is for your people to think you guided everyone to the decision you had already made. Those who have worked with you for any length of time will see through the charade. Better to say something along this line: "I have come up with what I think is a good solution [but don't let them know what it is at this point], but I want your ideas before I make the final decision."

Facilitators must then outline to their groups the details of the steps Define the Problem through Challenge Solutions explained in the next few pages.

Define the Problem

Einstein: "The formulation of a problem is far more often essential than its solution." A problem well defined is half solved. Doing so takes a lot of time, though.

> *Defining the problem may be the most important element in making*
>
> *effective decisions — and the one executives pay the least attention to.*
>
> *A wrong answer to the right problem can, as a rule, be repaired and*
>
> *salvaged. But the right answer to the wrong problem, that's very difficult*
>
> *to fix, if only because it's so difficult to diagnose. — Peter Drucker*

Before proceeding, answer this question: "Is this really the problem, or is it a symptom or part of a bigger problem?" This can't be underestimated. Often what appears to be the problem is just an indicator of a much larger dilemma.

Framing the definition of a problem as a question is the critical aspect of problem solving. As opposed to "We need to invest in this new product," reframe it as "Should we invest in this new product?" This assumes the quality question "Should we invest in new products?" has been answered. The reason the definition should be in question form is that answers will be challenged and tested as opposed to just confirmed. By asking a question, your people are best able to address the problem.

If the question is too broad, it will be impossible to answer. If it's too narrow, only part of the problem will be solved.

> *It is still a complex enterprise to get people to see the problem. — Bill Gates*

There will be three distinct definitions of the problem. One for each team. One definition will be neutral. One will be couched in terms of what can be gained. And one will highlight what can be lost. Usually, you'll find the solutions of the teams to be different depending on their definitions of the problem. Problems defined as potential gains tend to have more creative solutions. Problems defined as possible losses tend to have more traditional but risky solutions combined with a greater commitment of resources (Roberto). Problems defined as neutral fall between the other two.

The amateur poker player trying to decide whether to go pro.

Potential gain: How much can I win if I become a pro?
Possible loss: How much can I lose if I become a pro?
Neutral: Should I go pro?

The pharmaceutical company that has the potential to develop, at great expense, a breakthrough drug.

Potential gain: How many lives can we save with this new product?
Possible loss: How many lives will be lost without this new product?
Neutral: Should we invest in this new product?

The potential acquisition.

Potential gain: How much can we gain from this acquisition?
Possible loss: How much can we lose if we acquire this company?
Neutral: Should we acquire this company?

Most big decisions are binary, and each team needs to answer only one question; however, there can be times when the problem is so complex that a series of questions is necessary.

Should I fire the air traffic controllers? Reagan had to juggle considerations of safety, political ramifications, public reactions, the union — and many other moving parts. There were a number of options to "appease" the union that could have been considered. In the end, he stuck to his personal philosophy and fired them all. He promptly had military flight controllers fill the void until the union was busted.

If we knew what we were doing, it wouldn't be called research. — Albert Einstein

Separate things known from those unknown. List the facts pertaining to the problem. Filter evidence from conjecture. Again, if a team can figure out why something is happening, a potential answer often appears. Charles Knight, former chairman of Emerson Electric:

"Getting to the facts is the key to good decision making. Every mistake I made came because I wasn't smart enough to get the facts."

Also list assumptions and opinions. Each team member is to become an asker-in-chief, constantly asking "Why?" and "What if?"

Try to understand biases and emotions. This isn't as easy as it seems. All of us tend to project ourselves onto others. The honest person expects others to be honest. The thief thinks everyone else steals. Poker bluffers hate to fold because they assume their opponents are bluffing. Much bias is brought about by our culture, and culture is connected to history by repeating what has happened before. Our perceptions might or might not be right, but too often we accept a view because that's the way it's always been.

> *I had just been elected to a very prestigious board of directors for the International Health and Racquet Sports Association. At dinner that night, I proudly told the family, and my ego came out when I said, "I wonder how many great people there are in this industry?" Brian, fourteen at the time, didn't miss a bite of his burger as he said, "One less than you think."*

Research assumptions and opinions to see which can be changed into facts. Highly important. Too many crucial decisions are made with what were thought to be facts but turned out to be opinions. No WMD.

Challenge the experts, no matter how well qualified they are. Too many experts are often wrong but never in

> *Pride can make you play over your head rather than with it. — Lyle Berman*

doubt. Their air of "I know all" must be confronted. Most have hard-wired biases and don't accept the limitations of their own knowledge. Several of your management team members' thinking is as good as theirs, and probably better, since they will have a vision for your organization the outside experts won't have. Larry Ellison, CEO of Oracle: "The most important aspect of my personality has been my questioning conventional wisdom, doubting the experts, and questioning authority. While that can be very painful in relationships with your parents and teachers, it is enormously useful in life."

Experts often possess more data than judgment. Elites can become so inbred that they produce hemophiliacs who bleed to death as soon as they are nicked by the real world. — Colin Powell

Give equal weight to all knowledge regardless of when it was uncovered. Beware the tendency to give too great a weight to the information first (the anchor) or most recently discovered.

Also beware the status quo trap. Many individuals have great ideas, but they don't want to start anything. Many organizations coast along (there's only one direction you can go when you coast), and nothing gets done unless there's a crisis, and even when faced with an emergency, there are always those who are resistant to change. Buffett doesn't regret "commission — taking a risk and failing," but he laments "omission — not taking a risk and missing out on an opportunity."

Ignore sunk costs. Don't throw good money after bad. Once money is in the pot, it should not affect a decision. Lederer: "Whether to continue the business should strictly be one of how much time and how much money do I have to put into the business from here and what's my reward if things go well. What you have put into the pot is already gone. It should not affect your decision." Berman:

I know some poker players who cannot get away from a hand they are playing. They sense they are beaten, yet they continue to play out the hand, betting and losing more money, instead of folding and keeping their losses to a minimum. The same is true with business projects. At one time or another, all entrepreneurs have invested in a business that sputtered. What separates successful entrepreneurs from the rest is that they know when to pull the plug and stem the flow of red ink.

All are encouraged to listen carefully to opposing views and information. Everyone is to look for the error in their own truth and the truth in everyone else's error. Arimond: "Listen with a careful ear. Listen to both what they say and what they want you to hear but also what they don't say. Sometimes what they don't say is almost as important as what they do say." Phil Quillin, CEO of Quillin's Groceries: "Talk to a lot of people with knowledge. Find some people who have had experience facing the same types of things and get their honest opinions. There are a lot of people who are willing to share and willing to help."

It's always easier to listen to those who confirm your opinion than to get disconcerting information to help form your view. But Barry Rand of Xerox puts it well: "If you have a yes man working for you, one of you is redundant."

Determine the context of the decision. Which other decisions have been made that might influence this one? Which decisions might have to be made in the future because of this one? Some will call for action now. Figure out when the decision is really needed. And, if the problem is complex, can it be subdivided into smaller problems and thus smaller decisions?

Redefine the problem, again in the form of a question. The final definition should be as simple as possible. Loop around and around until the team is satisfied it has the best definition of the problem possible. The problem should be so well defined that everyone in the organization, from top to bottom, should be able to understand it.

Conduct a SWOT Analysis

SWOT, or *strengths*, *weaknesses*, *opportunities*, and *threats*, isn't very useful to your executives. If they don't have all of this in their heads, they should have been kicked off the bus long ago. But it's extremely useful to stakeholders and outside experts coming in to look at the problem. Each team is to independently conduct a SWOT analysis as it pertains to the problem at hand. A general analysis is of little value. One that focuses on the problem will be of great value to those outside your company (Kueffel).

The next few paragraphs are intentional restatements from previous sections since I realize some readers might have just skipped to this chapter.

Most strengths and weaknesses are analyzed for things beyond the organization's control, as shown earlier with the traditional marketing model: that is, price, product, place, promotion, people (employees), and finances.

Here your management team members will have all the information they need. It's just a matter of hunting and gathering, but they must ensure they list everything as it relates to the problem.

A partial analysis of Xcel Energy's SWOT looks like this.

Strengths (things somewhat under Xcel's control)
- Extensive transmission, distribution, and transportation structure
- Diversified customer base
- Strong financial performance

Weaknesses (things somewhat under Xcel's control)
- Coal-fired generation assets
- Lack of presence in upstream activities

Opportunities (things generally beyond Xcel's control)
- Increased demand for electricity
- Increasing natural gas business
- Competitors' investment in renewable energy

Threats (things generally beyond Xcel's control)
- Environment compliance costs
- Consolidation and joint ventures in the North American utility industry
- Government regulations

It might turn out that the analysis is nothing more than a restatement of the facts and assumptions your management team have already gathered, but putting them in the form of a SWOT analysis prompts the next step: potential solutions.

Come Up with Solutions

The first solution should always be to do nothing. Not every problem in the world must be solved. Many men die with prostate cancer, not because of it.

Then come up with out-of-the-box solutions. Wild-and-crazy-guy solutions. Not logical. Nothing is out of bounds. Combine and piggyback. A true brainstorming session. Push the group's thinking to the edge of their mental envelopes. Hire Irving to burn down the Walmart.

> *We can't solve problems by using the same kind of thinking*
> *we used when we created them.* — *Albert Einstein*

Before the era of ceiling cameras, a hardware store owner wanted to know where his customers spent most of their time when they shopped. As a customer arrived, he was given a bag of peanuts. At the end of the day, the store owner just looked to see where the biggest pile of peanut shells was (Foss).

Garrett Brown invented the Steadicam. It keeps the picture steady regardless of what happens to the camera. He used the same technology to invent "zero gravity" arms. This is an industrial robotic arm that attaches to heavy tools, making them essentially weightless for the user, all without inhibiting a tool's use. It uses only springs and requires no outside power. Ford, Boeing, and Deere are among the pioneers to use Zero G on their factory floors (Macht).

Frank Uhler, the former CEO of La Crosse Footwear, walked in and said he'd join my club if I could find someone to play racquetball with him. I'm customer oriented, so I told him I'd be happy to play. We became fast friends. Fast for men is in inverted dog years. It was over seven years before we said anything to one another other than the score.

After more than 30 years of playing each other, he came in and said he couldn't play anymore. I told him he never could. Then he said his cardiologist had told him he had a heart problem and would die if he kept playing racquetball. Using my out-of-the-box thinking skills, I told him there was only one solution — get another cardiologist. Frank stopped playing. He died a few months later.

Another approach is to find solutions that others have used to solve similar problems.

Last, come up with in-the-box solutions. Traditional solutions should come after out-of-the-box ones have been exhausted. As everyone's mind is stretched during the out-of-the-box exercise, traditional solutions become more numerous. One in-the-box solution is to acquire instead of build. Instead of trying to develop its own online system, Walgreens purchased drugstore.com to enter the online prescription market (Reineke).

Put Each Solution to an Ethics Test

This test assumes that we know what is ethical. In the What Guides Us model, we see that our moral standards form the base for our ethical behavior. Morals are the base. The law is what is required by society. Etiquette is what is expected by society.

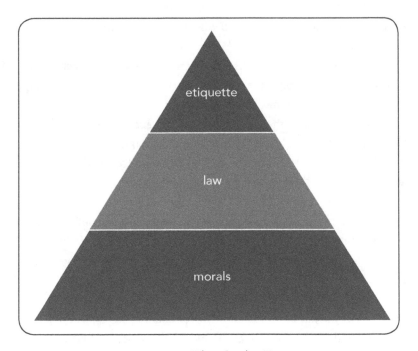

Figure 5.3 What Guides Us

Just because it's a law doesn't make it moral. A convicted child molester applied for a job in my day care. My attorney advised me that I couldn't refuse to hire the molester, because he had served his time. When I told the applicant that I'd rather close the day care than comply with the law, he left and never came back. Fortunately, the law has since been changed.

You see someone right after an accident, and it's obvious he needs help right away. You know there isn't a Good Samaritan law in your state, and if he's hurt while you try to help him, you could face a big lawsuit. We all know what we must do.

How about conscience? It's our inner voice. It comes from a combination of heredity, how one was raised by his parents, and his culture's customs. But parents and cultures are often ignorant about some things and prejudiced about others. How about religion? For those who are deeply religious, their answers might be clear but have the same drawbacks as parental upbringing or culture.

Here are the ethics tests I use in my classes. Yes, they are too simple, but they do have value.

Test 1. I ask how many in the class believe in God. For those who do believe in God, it's easy to make a principled choice as long as the person understands any built-in prejudice in his religion.

Test 2. I then ask how many aren't sure about God or don't believe in God. This is always the majority. I give this group two filters. First I ask them to assume the person they care about most in the world, living or dead, is watching them. Would that person be proud of their decision? Then I ask them to assume that whatever decision they make will be plastered on the Internet the next day for the whole world to see.

Test 3. Is it fair or unfair? Right or wrong? Good or bad? Is this an excellent way to live our lives?

Now eliminate every solution that doesn't pass anyone's ethics test. This is a time for absolutes, no grays. Krzyzewski: "There are clear lines of right and wrong."

Have utmost concern with what's right. Ability may get you to the top, but character keeps you there. — *John Wooden*

Determine Future Consequences

Of course, it's presumptuous to think this is possible. No one really knows what we are setting in motion, what the consequences will be, both intended and unintended, both short term and long term, but everyone must still do their best even if the perfect is unattainable.

The first consequence is required resources. We list not only the resources necessary for each solution but also an accounting of cost and time to obtain those resources.

Many solutions include redundancy, which costs more but usually proves to be a wise investment once action takes place. Redundancy allows us to use every weapon we have. Wherever possible, a redundant system or structure should be completely independent of the other systems or structures. When solving critical problems, we can't just do one thing, we must do everything.

For every action, there is an equal and opposite reaction. Anticipate the reaction. Unforeseen reactions usually mean trouble.

If the firm is profit driven, put faces to dollars. When seven consumers died after taking Tylenol that had been tampered with, the CEO, James Burke, recalled every bottle. An extremely expensive move. Sales of Tylenol fell sharply. But he did the right thing. Ultimately, the company benefited by regaining market share and customer trust (Fritz).

Consequences include payoffs. We discussed payoffs in the chapter on knowledge. Recall that payoffs can be not just in dollars but also include psychological detriments or benefits.

Separate short-term and long-term consequences. What are the moral hazards? The unintended consequences? We can sell an inferior product because we can purchase it at little cost from a foreign manufacturer that is dumping inventory. Short term we will make a profit; long term our image in terms of quality and social responsibility will be hurt.

There is a lot that is unseen. We see the jobs created by the tax-funded stadium but don't see the revenue and hours lost by other businesses.

Imagine not just intended but also unintended consequences. Our printing company could make a nice profit from the new child porn account. How would our employees feel if we accepted this order? Would some quit? Would we be encouraging more child abuse? What would happen to our image in the community? And so on.

Consider ethanol, the biofuel as an additive for gas. As a form of renewable energy, it was mandated by several governments with good intentions.

But what happened? Those who raise livestock were forced to compete with the ethanol plants for corn, resulting in higher corn prices, fewer livestock, and higher meat prices. As the supply of food was reduced, prices for food increased dramatically worldwide, impacting the poorest the most. As the world adopts ethanol, almost 20% of all agricultural land will be devoted to fuel production. And, since it takes so much energy to convert the renewable source to fuel, carbon emissions are on the rise.

Which forces, competitive or otherwise, can prevent a solution? Just as in a poker hand, the meta-game begins. If this affects a competitor, anticipate what he will do. Then what you will do if he does X, Y. Then what he will do. Then what you will do. Then what he will do. And so on.

More questions.

- What are the critical success factors, those few explicit things that must go right, for the solution to work (Bullen and Rockart)?
- How do the critical success factors affect stakeholders? They include family, customers, employees and their families, stockholders, boards of directors, bosses, lenders, vendors, community, government, environmental, social, political, religious, and non-adversarial competitors.
- Which solutions result in either a real or a perceived conflict of interest?
- Which forces will assist or hinder the solution?

Identify the capabilities needed for each solution. Consider the resources necessary in the future. As mentioned earlier, it often costs more to hold on to an objective than it took to reach it.

Now cost/benefit analysis. Some things can be quantified; for example, we have to invest $100,000, and we think we'll make $20,000 a year. Many things can't. They usually have long term costly consequences. They involve fuzzy things such as reputation, brand image, value, customer satisfaction, employee fulfillment, government licenses and regulations.

After a tornado, a town was inundated with non-local contractors who did shoddy repairs, took money, and left town. The ethical contractors' reputations suffered since the newspaper stories made it sound as if all were crooked. The politicians responded with a raft of new regulations, impacting every contractor.

Challenge Each Remaining Solution

Use charts, diagrams, decision trees, models. Test every solution. Where possible, use math to isolate variables when testing. Use game theory, probability, operations research, computer modeling, artificial intelligence, or any of the other forms of technological insight. Always remember, math is a great tool both in poker and in business, but it's not as precise as it appears.

When our children were growing up, every so often Carol and I would have role reversal day. Our children never knew in advance when that day would be. They became the parents ("Clean up your room"), and we became the children ("No"). A meal prepared by a six year old is something to behold. It was very interesting to see how they handled leadership for the first time in their lives. I used this in one of my health club businesses. Everyone switched roles now and then. I was maintenance; one of the day care managers worked in accounting; the accounting person ran the club. A great learning experience for all.

How does this apply to challenging solutions? Without warning, everyone who has been a proponent — executives, stakeholders, outside experts, and those with specialized knowledge — must now become an opponent and vice versa. This technique often points out leaks in our thinking.

Pick a Solution

Now each team is ready to present its solution to the other two teams in attendance with you. Once each team has seen other solutions, it's free to change its own solution. Be careful not to give away your feelings about any solution, for most of your executive team members will lean the way they think you do. If you want to share your opinion, do it with your dog, not your parrot. Then meet privately with each person and ask, "Regardless of your team's decision, if you were me, what would you do and why?" Thank each individual.

Now use the old Ben Franklin technique. Evaluate the pros and cons of each solution. Rate the rewards, risks, and costs of each. Rank them. Then pick one.

Of course, your solution won't be perfect, but the more information and knowledge you have, the more you have followed the process so far, the more you will see things as they are and not as you wish them to be. You are now ready to pick the most logical solution.

If a lot of time has passed, see if any of your original facts or assumptions has changed. New information and alternatives come with time.

Then make your decision.

When you pick a solution, never assume that everyone concurs with it. Many will remain silent even though they don't agree. See who confirms your solution. See who dissents.

> *Great leaders are almost always great simplifiers, who can offer a*
> *solution everybody can understand. — Colin Powell*

When I was in the Army, I noticed that the best generals would, before an order was issued, let a private read it. If the private couldn't understand the order, it had to be rewritten.

> *If words of command are not clear and distinct, if orders are not*
> *thoroughly understood, the general is to blame. — Sun Tzu*

When Carol came back from the hospital, her foot was heavily bandaged after the operation. Joe, age two, was unbelievably happy to have Mom back home. As he ran to hug her, he stepped on her foot. Carol, holding back a scream through tears of pain, said, "Oh, Joe, you stepped on the wrong foot." He looked up. Seeing how upset and hurt Carol was, he did the only thing he thought she wanted. He stepped on her other foot.

Check details carefully. Since the road to the solution has been so long, often the fine points are glossed over. Many get caught up in the formality of the process. *Vigilance* is the word.

Pick a plan B. If plan A doesn't work, make sure you can pull your plan B off the shelf and be ready to go. The same for a plan C and D.

Secure Stakeholder Buy-In

Spock wouldn't think of getting his stakeholders' buy-in because so far everything has been logical, even the vigorous debate. That's his leak.

The next sentence contains one of the most important concepts in this book. *Your solution might be like your newborn baby, uglier than you think.*

If you have selected your decision team members carefully, you should have representatives of those stakeholders most affected already informed. They might not agree with the final decision, but they should agree that the process has been fair and equitable.

The best condition is when your thoughtful creation is embraced by the stakeholders most affected. That's full buy-in. You'll then have tribal behavior on your side. Performance is directly related to buy-in. You can't lead if no one will follow.

LBJ did a masterful job of getting the politicians on board but neglected how the public would react. And that was his downfall. Big lesson.

I wish I'd understood this in my early business career. I was constantly making deals and taking tremendous entrepreneurial risks, borrowing millions for my health clubs, without getting Carol's buy-in because I thought I knew it all and could do it all on my own. Wrong.

So how do you get buy-in? Just like the elephant feast, one bite at a time. The more the stakeholders are affected, the more time they need to see how you went about making the decision. Explain the process and who was involved. Explain the various options and how you made the decision. Explain how the decision fits in with the vision and mission.

If there is enough time, let all of those affected tell you their opinions. When the stakeholders buy in, they become more invested in your course of action, resulting in commitment, action, and, most importantly, implementation. Once the battle starts, those on the ground will determine success or failure.

If the stakeholders can't embrace the decision, the next best thing is their acceptance. What do you do if you can't even gain acceptance? Critical decisions won't be embraced or even accepted by everyone. Powell: "Good leadership involves responsibility to the welfare of the group, which means that some people will get angry at your actions and decisions. It's inevitable, if you're honorable." Few people like surprises, except on their birthdays. At a minimum, prepare your stakeholders for what's coming. Figure 5.4 illustrates these concepts.

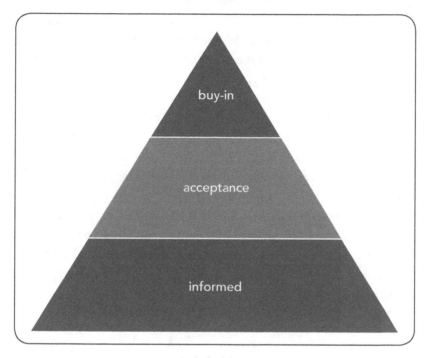

Figure 5.4 Stakeholder Reception

There is a con to getting stakeholder buy-in or preparing your stakeholders for what's coming. It takes time. The more delays there are, the more events will change. Nothing stands still.

Sometimes you can predict the window will slam shut if you don't seize the moment. You needn't be the mushy consensus cooperator conciliator. For sure, you never want to get into the university model of self-governance, where it literally takes years to implement a good idea and every formal statement is an exercise in trying to please everyone.

Reflect on Your Decision

So far all the steps have been designed to give you clarity. But, more importantly, you must have peace.

There is power in reflective time. Sleep on it. If you have the time, reflect on your decision for several days. Can you say, "Based on what we know at this time, are we probably right"? Does it fit with your intuition? Even though the process has been detailed, ensure it makes sense and feels right. It goes back to your compass. Decisions are easier if you know who you are. Does this decision support your beliefs, your life's purpose?

One technique I have found helpful is to dwell on a cherished moment having nothing to do with the problem. It could be a time spent with a child, perhaps fishing. Another technique is a long, slow walk around a secluded lake with your dog. Perhaps some music or a particular smell that brings you back to a quiet place in your mind or another moment in time, where you can observe yourself without judgment.

As you watch the best poker players, you see that most seldom make hasty decisions. They first analyze all of the information they have available as objectively and realistically as possible and then act depending on their intuition. Wasicka: "I process all of the information, all of the numbers, but when it comes down to it, it's all about inside, do I feel good about making the decision? I ultimately go with my instincts." Berman, when creating the World Poker Tour: "I went with my gut." Paraphrasing Johnny Cochran, if the logic says yes, and your heart says no, you cannot go.

> *Don't fall victim to the ready-aim-aim-aim syndrome.*
> *You must be willing to fire.* — *T. Boone Pickens*

Pull the Trigger

The turtle makes progress only when he sticks his neck out. Hill: "Knowledge is only potential power." The greatest thinking is worth nothing without action. You must be willing to act on what you know; you must be willing to pull the trigger. Powell:

> *You miss 100% of the shots you don't take.* — *Wayne Gretzky*

"You can encourage participative management and bottom-up employee involvement, but ultimately the essence of leadership is the willingness to make the tough, unambiguous choices that will have an impact on the fate of the organization. Harry Truman was right. Whether you're a

CEO or the temporary head of a project team, the buck stops here." Truman was an avid poker player who used to call the button the buck. The saying "the buck stops here" meant he was the last person to act after he had all the information.

> *So often in life we don't do things because we're afraid of failure.*
> *You might lose now and then, but if you don't play the game and take*
> *action you never have a chance of success. — Sean Duffy*

The quality of your decision can only be measured at the moment when you act, based on the information you have. Your decisions will seldom, if ever, be perfect. And you'll never know if they were perfect, regardless of the outcomes. Some might call it analysis, but it's just a best guess. No absolutes here, just grays.

Get it. Get it done. Get it done right. Get it done right now!

Evaluate, Experiment, and Adapt

Your great plan will have milestones and checkpoints along the way. Nice, but they don't have much to do with the reality of the moment. No battle plan ever survives contact with the enemy.

Your plan will evolve. But, more than likely, you'll have little to no influence over the dice you have thrown. Your people will experiment. We'll try this and see what happens. Once things start to happen, you lose whatever command you thought you had. The moment is controlled by those in the trenches.

We all make mistakes when making decisions. Kissinger's advice is best: "If it's going to come out eventually, better have it come out immediately." Forget rolling disclosure. Let it all come out. This is not just part of leadership; it helps everyone to adapt.

Remember that step about stakeholder buy-in? The concept that we want the tribe not just to be with us but also to *want* to be with us. As stated in the introduction, leadership is all about creating the environment in which anyone in your organization makes the same decision and takes the same action you would if you were there giving him the freedom to do so.

Critical Decision Summary

A single decision is not likely to kill the business even if you are dreadfully wrong. — Joe Chilsen

Use the Decision-Making model in Figure 5.2 (page 183) as a checklist, but know that there is a lot we don't know. Although the process is important, don't get caught up in the formality of it. The model looks good, but we don't live in a simple cause-and-effect world. No model is complete or static.

Realize that most decisions are a crapshoot. Once the cards are dealt, the result is only as good as the environment you have created. As always, know that the model isn't close to reality. Nothing is done from one step to another. It is diverge, converge, somewhere in between, then more iterations. There are always ideas, facts, opinions, solutions, consequences that are added, deleted, in no real order. Figure 5.5 sums it up.

There are no right answers. There is no such thing as perfect play.
— Howard Lederer

Even after everything is done, too often we aren't sure why we were successful. We probably will never know if we chose the best path. If the outcome is good, we enjoy our brief moment in the sun. Greg Raymer, Pfizer attorney and WSOP main event champion: "The thing that poker teaches you is to focus on the quality of decisions you make and really to ignore the results as much as possible."

Each success only buys an admission ticket to a more difficult problem.
— Henry Kissinger

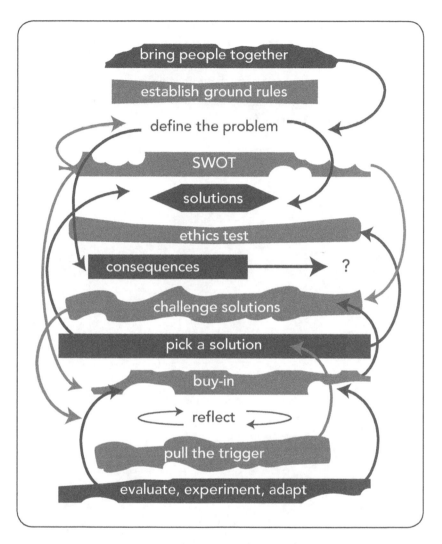

Figure 5.5 Decision-Making Reality

With every medicine comes a little poison. The poison of using the Spock Decision-Making model is that it takes time. A lot of it. By now you probably think, if you follow everything I suggest, you'll never get anything done. This adage, which sits on Philip Gelatt's desk, prevails in almost every situation: "A good plan violently executed now is far better than the perfect plan implemented next week." Powell: "Don't wait until you have enough facts to be 100% sure. Today, excessive delays in the name of information gathering breed analysis paralysis. Procrastination in the name of reducing risk actually increases risk." He who hesitates is last. Warp seven, Mr. Sulu.

If you use this model and something goes wrong, it's easy to go back in your after-action review and see exactly what went wrong so you don't make the same mistake in the future.

6

Baking It In

To get the hive going in the same direction, we must not just sprinkle empowerment on top of our corporate culture. It must be baked in from bottom to top.

There is one sure-fire way to destroy any organization. Just have your staff do what you tell them to do and nothing more. Rules grind down great people and eventually grind them out. No matter how detailed your procedures, if you don't give your people the freedom to make decisions, you are doomed. Politicians need to understand this too. Regulations grind down great companies and sometimes even great leaders.

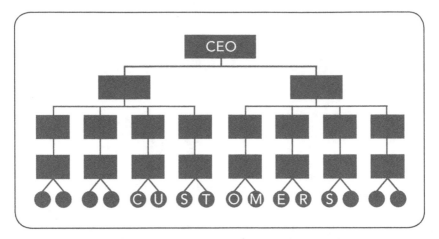

Figure 6.1 Traditional Organizational Chart

If people really followed organization charts, companies would collapse.
— Colin Powell

We all know the traditional organization chart. You are on top, your staff below (Figure 6.1). I suggest you consider formally turning your organization chart upside down — for all to see. Once that occurs, your customers become the most important, the staff who deal directly with them (sales and service) turn out to be your most important employees (and the most knowledgeable about transitioning customers' needs), and your executive staff and you realize that your job is to give your people the proper environment to serve your customers (Figure 6.2). The leader becomes the servant, other-centered as opposed to self-centered. Noyce: "When your people want to master their position, it is up to the CEO to give them the tools and resources to do it."

A benefit to this type of organization is that most decisions are made on the line or by middle management. Many important proposed courses of action "trickle down" from the organization to the CEO.

As our economy has made the shift from agriculture to manufacturing to service, there has been an increased need for social capital: that is, for people to get along with each other. "From a business model and leadership perspective, we're seeing a massive shift from management by command and control to management by collaboration and teamwork" (Chambers).

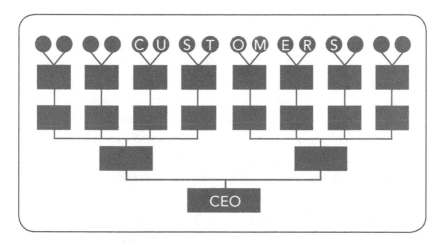

Figure 6.2 Customer Employee Organizational Chart

If you are going to achieve excellence in big things, you develop the habit in little matters. Excellence is not an exception, it is a prevailing attitude. — Colin Powell

Habits completely control our minds and bodies. The right habits = success. That's pretty simple. Simple things work. I've seen studies saying that it takes three weeks to develop a habit. I don't buy it. My experience is that it takes two to six months of patient repetition before something gradually becomes part of the subconscious and turns into a lifelong habit. If you disagree, wait until

You first form your habits, and then your habits form you. The rule is that good habits are hard to form but easy to live with. Bad habits are easy to form but hard to live with. And everything in life is a habit. — Brian Tracy

you have a two year old going through potty training. And it works best if we develop one habit at a time.

I know that everyone's greatest treasure is time. Tomorrow you'll wake up and be 90 years old. I'm asking you to give me 10 minutes of every day for the next six months. You can read this book in a few hours. But thinking in a strategic way involves repetition until it becomes routine, effortless, part of your everyday life. *Kaizen* — small, continuous improvements — comes naturally the more you use it. And, the more you use it, the easier it becomes. You'll get to a point where you don't even think about it.

Remember that discussion about finding your compass? During your journey of discovery, you might find emotions in conflict with your good angel. We talked about a simple, time-tested way for you to change your emotions. Fake it until you make it. During the next few months, make a daily effort to change a specific part of your behavior. Visualize exactly what your behavior should be, and then act that way. Write it down. Look at it and repeat it every day. As long as that change lines up with what you are discovering about your inner self, your emotions will change, unhur- riedly, gradually, and the change will become permanent. Once that change is done, go on to another behavior you want to improve.

Give 110% effort all the time to what's important in your life. Efficiency is doing things right; effectiveness is finding the right things to do (Drucker). We all need to find the right things to do first before we do them right. Many students think they can turn it on when they get their first jobs. It's too late then. By that time, either they have developed the habit of giving their best, or they haven't.

Luke, in the movie *Cool Hand Luke*, finally said, "My mind is right, boss." How do we get our minds right every day?

Way back on the first few pages we talked about creating an atmosphere in which your people are so engaged in what they are doing they will act as if they are you and in some cases, better than you would. Your corporate culture is a disease that everyone catches. It's the way the people in your organization think, do things, make decisions, and take care of problems. Fortunately, you have the power to create the disease.

If everyone consistently pursues looking into the future and acting on what he sees, both the collective purpose and the energies of the hive are freed. The worker bees, not the queen bee, decide on the location of the new hive. Happy bees mean a happy hive.

In most organizations, everyone feels as if he's just a passenger on the bus. In your organization, you want him to feel as though he has a hand on the wheel.

Each person should have the feeling that he can influence what happens. The earlier and more involved everyone is in every step of thinking strategically, acquiring knowledge, and making decisions, the more he feels as if he's part of a real team. Let your people state their opinions, and listen to their ideas. Delegating, allowing participation, encouraging them to think of their own solutions to problems (Guiffre). Really turning the organization chart upside down. Creating and keeping a transparent business culture (Fritz). All of this keeps your organization moving from "They did it" to "We did it" (Pisapia), and eventually the distinction disappears. When your organization is driven by a shared commitment, a cause, a purpose, a conviction, an identification with those who believe what you believe (Sinek), it becomes "We did it."

Below is the start-of-the-day routine I recommend for everyone in your organization, no matter what his job. It's the equivalent of a great artist giving a wall to his child and telling him he can put anything on that wall he wants — it's the child's wall. If you think some of this is corny, try it for six months. I think you'll be amazed at the results.

Before we go through the list, when I say "handwrite," I don't mean on a keyboard. I mean pen and paper. There is a psychological connection between your brain and your eye seeing something permanent (that's why a pen is used) in your own handwriting that results in a great deal of selective attention and action. (Some schools don't teach handwriting anymore. Students go directly to a keyboard. Big mistake for their futures.)

All items on the list are voluntary. The first five are private to the individual and are not for public consumption.

1. Using meditation, visualize where you are going with your life.
2. Write down your personal mission statement.
3. Write down the 10 most important things you can do today to help you with your personal mission. Then circle the top two (most important, not most urgent).

4. Compare the most important things you said you could do yesterday with what you actually accomplished.

5. Audio-record yourself stating your personal affirmations, such as "I am happy," "I am healthy," "I have a wonderful family," "I will accomplish the most important thing I can do today" (Tracy). They are said enthusiastically (yes, rah, rah), with a true smile. By the time you read this, there will be even more technological possibilities than a privately created YouTube audio or video for this daily reaffirmation. The how doesn't matter. Doing it does.

6. See the company's vision, perhaps on a YouTube or similar video. Best if this is done by the employee himself, or a fellow employee (perhaps on a rotating basis), but at a minimum by the leader.

> *Our greatest power is the freedom to choose. We decide what we do, what we think, and where we go. We can do what we want to do. We can be who we want to be. We develop our own future by applying persistence to the possibilities. Our future is all around us. If we see, we will find it. If the door is closed, we must knock and keep knocking until it opens. We never give up. — Cirulli's Customer Service Manual*

The following items should be on some company-wide secure social network, blog, or forum where ideas and comments can be posted either anonymously or by the author. Today, with networking, it's the power of mass collaboration. If you pool together all that knowledge through the use of this technology, you get much better ideas than any one person can generate. It allows people to come together in a way in which they don't need to know with whom they are collaborating. They can be anonymous to one another, but they can work together (Roberto).

1. Write down and post the most important thing you will do today to help us accomplish our company's mission.

2. Compare what you said was the most important thing yesterday with what you actually accomplished yesterday.

3. Here is a situation we are facing (this will be a current opportunity or problem). Do you have any thoughts? Cisco received over 1,000 ideas by allowing anyone in the world to submit his thoughts on future technology.

4. Here is what we are considering doing (this will be a course of action you have tentatively decided on for a specific opportunity or problem). Do you have any thoughts? All of John Deere's employees complete monthly surveys on how the company is performing and whether anything could be improved. Weekly meetings are held where employees can share thoughts about the business (Hubner).

5. Is there anything else you'd like to contribute to achieve our vision and mission?

Several of the above lead to decisions made throughout the day, while others offer opportunities for involvement and empowerment. Each decision made is more important than most realize. Some decisions might seem small at the time, but the reality is that they add to one another to become habits that move us with increasing force toward some destiny. A contagion, a domino effect. That destiny is your personal vision and your company's vision. If they converge, then both you and your company benefit. Organizations that offer involvement and empowerment result in potential buy-in, things they haven't considered, and ideas no one else has thought of.

Doctors know that when you improve one part of the body, other parts are improved. Lowering cholesterol reduces the likelihood of getting prostate cancer. They understand that everything is linked, but they don't yet understand the exact connections.

I don't claim to know exactly how everything is interrelated, but I do know that, when your spiritual, mental, social, and physical parts are in harmony, you will play with more confidence. Everything we have gone over is designed to help you make decisions with more self-assurance. More confidence leads to a positive mental mindset, which leads to greater performance. As belief in self increases, expectations of success increase. Superior confidence, short of arrogance, leads to superior performance.

There is no reason to wait. Today is the tomorrow we worried about yesterday. All of these habits can be established now on your own turf. The little engine that could was right all along.

7

Conclusion

By now you know my view that there is no silver bullet, but there is silver buckshot.

Playing poker, we must learn to view everything through the eyes of others, remain cool under fire, evaluate numbers and probabilities, make the best of limited resources, manage our money, respond to various personalities, project changing conditions, work with imperfect information, analyze the situation as best we can, make a calculated decision, then act and adapt. These are the same skills necessary for business leaders.

Which models are important? If I had to pick three, I'd say Strategic-Thinking, Knowledge, and Decision-

Making (Figures 2.1, page 30; 3.1, page 59; and 5.2, page 183, respectively). But none can be taken in isolation. They are interdependent, intertwined, and no isolated part should ever be used alone.

My top-10 list.

1. Get into the skin of others. Find their truths. Treat everyone the way he wants to be treated.
2. The two most important days in your life are the day you were born and the day you discover why you were born.
3. Listening builds trust. Careful active listening builds lasting trust.
4. Most winners are good people.
5. The F word — *fun*. Winners laugh every day.
6. Leadership is all about creating an environment in which anyone in your organization makes the same decision and takes the same action you would if you were there. And it's about giving him the freedom to do so. The environment is created by letting everyone know why he's doing what he's doing and then painting a picture of where the company is going and letting each person see where he fits in that picture.
7. Time is your most precious asset. You will wake up tomorrow and be 90 years old.
8. Launch, keep moving, keep learning, keep getting experience, stay positive by using the daily routine for getting your mind right.
9. Clarity and peace let you make the wisest decision possible, even though it will never be perfect. To arrive at clarity, use the best information you have at the time to understand what is going on around you. To achieve peace, make sure it feels right.
10. When we die, we need to be proud of how we interacted with our families and how we played our lives.

The boardroom table and the poker table. The only difference between them is a layer of felt. At these tables, we go all-in, are fully leveraged. Reading risks and rewards here isn't much different from reading them on a spreadsheet. We play because poker is like business, without the conference calls. The office might close at 6 p.m., but there is a game that is always open. This paraphrased commercial by defunct Full Tilt isn't far off the mark.

> *The "board" in "boardroom" comes from early meetings of those in charge of a business. They would put a big board on some sawhorses and pull their chairs up to it.*

Did I get it right? Of course not, but I tried to. I attempted to convey the thoughts of the very best, to show how things hang together, how one element relates to another, and to translate the reflective into the practical. I'm sure there are leaks in my thinking, examples I have missed, or thoughts from those more experienced I have left out. I'd like future editions to be vessels for more ideas. If you see anything that needs correction or elaboration, or if you have some personal history that would help future readers and students, please contact me at TheSharkAndTheFish@gmail.com.

Best,

An old Christmas card. From left to right, top: Brian, Joe; bottom: Chuck, Carol, Charley.

Acknowledgments

Although I am responsible for everything in this book, and for everything missed, I do need to thank those who helped me to complete it. Tom Hench's insightful thoughts appear liberally in the introduction. A very special thanks to Brian Swayne, Adam Macht, Dan Rosenblatt, Ryan Huinker, Dallas Harrison, and Jack David, who reviewed many of the chapters and gave me their thoughts. Thanks to George Arimond, who allowed me to create the course that became the basis for this book. Thanks also to the following.

Alan Bigel   Tiffany Le
Crissy Boylan   Bruce May
Steve Brokaw   Brian Mulrennan
Joe Chilsen   James Murray
Janet Craig   Emily Newell
Lise Graham   Ron Rubens
Jerry Krause

APPENDIX B

Playing Texas Hold'em

....

By Adam Macht

Texas Hold'em is a challenging game that takes a lifetime to master, but the basics can easily be learned. The following is an overview of how to play the game.

Texas Hold'em is a seven-card poker game in which each player is dealt two cards face down — his *hole cards* — and there are five *community cards* that each player uses. The goal is to make the best five-card poker hand using any combination of community and hole cards.

Hand rankings are as follows.

Straight flush
Four of a kind
Full house
Flush
Straight
Three of a kind
Two pair
Pair
High card

Poker is a game of patience. The *blinds* induce betting to keep the game moving. The player to the left of the dealer is the *small blind*; the player two to the left of the dealer is the *big blind*. Other players must match the big blind bet or any additional bets to stay in the hand. Typically, the minimum bet is equal to that of the big blind.

In a tournament, the blinds are raised on regular intervals by a pre-determined amount. A rule of thumb is that the big blind should start at

⅟₅₀th of each player's beginning chip stack. Without the blinds, players would sit around and play only premium hands, slowing down the game. The blinds ensure that the game finishes in a timely manner. An example of a blind structure for a game starting with 1,000 chips is as follows, with each new round starting every 15 minutes.

Round 1: 10, 20
Round 2: 20, 40
Round 3: 25, 50
Round 4: 50, 100
Round 5: 100, 200
Round 6: 150, 300
Round 7: 200, 400

In a cash game, the blinds typically remain constant. They are a good way to gauge how much money you should sit down with at the table, and there are many schools of thought on the amount. Often there is a maximum amount, but a good general rule is to sit down with at least 100 times the big blind. For example, if you are playing at a 5/10¢ table, it's best to sit down with at least $10.

The dealer shuffles the deck of cards and deals them face down one at a time until each player has two cards. The player immediately to the left of the dealer posts the small blind. The next player to the left posts twice as many chips and is the big blind.

Each player looks at his cards. The action begins with the player to the left of the big blind (three players to the left of the dealer). This position is called *under the gun*. Based on his hand, each player has the option to call the big blind, bet more chips, or fold. To remain in the hand, each player must call the blind or any bet made by another player. If the player doesn't think he has a chance to win the hand, he should fold. The betting goes clockwise around the table.

Once it has been determined how many people are in the hand, the dealer *burns* (discards) one card (it helps to ensure that the card is random) and deals three community cards — the *flop*. Another round of betting then takes place starting with the first player to the left of the dealer.

After the flop and the round of betting, the dealer burns another card and deals one more community card — the *turn*. Another round of betting then takes place.

Finally, the dealer burns one more card and deals the final community card — the *river*. The last round of betting then takes place. If any players still haven't folded, they now show their hands. Using any combination of the two hole cards and the five community cards, the best five-card poker hand wins the pot.

In tournament play, each player starts with the same amount of chips. The players then play against each other and battle increasing blinds to determine the winner. The last player remaining in the tournament is the winner.

A cash game is structured much like tournament play, except that the blinds are usually fixed. In this type of play, a player can play for as long as he likes and leave the table at his convenience.

Charley's Background

I've spent about 40% of my professional life as a business owner, 30% as a teacher, 10% writing, 10% consulting, and 10% as a professional speaker.

I was a captain in the Army from 1967 to 1970. In 1974, I started up a tennis and health club in La Crosse, Wisconsin. All my children grew up in the club, and my understanding wife, Carol, helped me with the business. The club closed in 2007. We helped over 30,000 residents live longer and healthier, and it was a pleasure to serve the community.

I have undergraduate degrees in mechanical engineering and business administration from Virginia Tech and a master's degree in business from the University of Utah.

One of my passions is teaching, and I consider myself a lifelong learner. At the university level, I have taught mathematics, statistics, economics, industrial engineering, marketing, finance, critical thinking, strategic thinking, supervision, leadership, total quality management, operations research, and ethics. I have presented seminars and taught at the University of Michigan, Virginia Tech, Radford University, Upper Iowa University, Viterbo University, Michigan State, Babson College, Lake Forest College, and University of Toronto. I teach at both graduate and undergraduate levels at Winona State and the University of Wisconsin–La Crosse. I have taught at the World Series of Poker Academy camps in Las Vegas and have a pre-recorded online poker course with some of the world's top poker players. I've been honored to receive emeritus status from the University of Wisconsin–La Crosse and the Excellence in Teaching Award from Upper Iowa.

I have created a rigorous, demanding, year-long program for those who want to become top-notch decision makers or poker players. My consulting and professional speaking have been in the areas of business startup, expansion, strategic thinking, and decision making.

My other books are on entrepreneurship, the stock market, advice to college students, creating a life plan, and poker, and I've authored about 100 magazine articles.

I have a wonderful wife (been married almost 50 years), great children, and lots of grandchildren. Carol is the perfect wife (also a great dancer and a black belt — I'm neither). We have three sons. Chuck played on the professional tennis tour and is now a property investor and manager. Brian is a former Navy fighter pilot and Wall Street equities trader (his two favorite movies are *Top Gun* and *Wall Street*). And Joe ran the family business for over 10 years (also a many-degreed black belt) and has owned his own karate studio.

On weekends, I'm at a cabin high above the Mississippi, with a spectacular view of critters (foxes, deer, turkeys, eagles) and the river, and either classical music or Elvis is playing in the background.

You can reach me by snail mail at N 1964 Crestview Place, La Crosse, WI, 54601, USA, or my email is TheSharkAndTheFish@gmail.com.

People Quoted and Sources Used

···

If you steal from one author, that's plagiarism.

If you steal from many, it's research. — *Wilson Mizner*

Many of the quotations or sources in the book are those I have used in class for many years. Sometimes I would hear or see something and write down the substance, if not the exact quotation, and who said it. Sometimes I didn't write down the name of the book or article. And some are just from memory, which is faulty. I emailed many to confirm what has been written, without success. For these reasons, there are leaks in this appendix. If you find a misquotation or a source not properly cited, it wasn't intentional. Contact me, and I'll make revisions in future editions.

Achilles: A Greek mythological hero in the Trojan wars.

Amrein, Jeff: CEO of Amber Platform Technologies and owner of Hog Wild Poker.

Arimond, George: Business owner, consultant, and department chair at the University of Wisconsin–La Crosse.

Aristotle: His writings cover physics, metaphysics, poetry, theater, music, and logic.

Ballmer, Steve: CEO of Microsoft.

Beal, Andy: Founder and chairman of Beal Bank and Beal Aerospace Technologies; known for his high-stakes, heads-up poker play.

Beinoff, Marc: Created Salesforce.com.

Bellande, Jean-Robert: Finisher at many final tables, with over $1.1 million in winnings.

Berman, Lyle: CEO of many businesses, founder of the World Poker Tour, and three-time bracelet winner.

Bon-Joon, Koo: CEO of LG Electronics.

Bonnie and Clyde: Bonnie Parker and Clyde Barrow, robbers and criminals.

Boone, Louis E. and David L. Kurtz: Authors of *Contemporary Marketing*.

Borg, Bjorn: Considered to be one of the greatest tennis players of all time. Winner of 11 Grand Slam singles titles and five consecutive Wimbledon singles titles.

www.brainyquote.com.

Brito, Carlos: CEO of Anheuser-Busch.

Brown, Garrett: Invented the Steadicam and zero gravity arms.

Brunson, Doyle: Winner of 10 WSOP bracelets and considered a legend in the poker industry.

Buffett, Warren: Regarded as one of the most successful investors in the world. More importantly, he has pledged to give away 99% of his fortune.

Bullen and Rockart: "A Primer on Critical Success Factors," Sloan School of Management, 1981.

Burke, James: Tylenol CEO.

www.businessweek.com.

Cardoza, Avery: CEO of Cardoza publishing, the world's leader in poker books.

Caro, Mike: Professional poker player and author.

Chambers, John: Cisco CEO.

Chan, Johnny: Back-to-back winner of the WSOP and holder of 10 bracelets.

Chauhan, Sam: A mindset coach and CEO of Changing You.

Chilsen, Joe: Good friend, turn-around expert, and world-class teacher.

Cirulli, Joe: Good friend, owns the Gainesville Health and Fitness Center. You might have seen him on the cover of *Inc.* magazine.

Clay, Cassius: Later became Muhammad Ali, regarded as the best boxer ever.

Click and Clack brothers: Tom and Ray Magliozzi, also known as the Tappet brothers, have a weekly show on PBS called *Car Talk*.

Cline, Charlie: Poker player and friend.

Clinton, Bill: 42nd president of the United States.

Cochran, Johnny: Lawyer best known for defending O.J. Simpson.

Collins, Jim: Co-author with Jerry Porass of *Built to Last*.

Confucius: A Chinese thinker and social philosopher who emphasized personal and governmental morality, correctness of social relationships, justice, and sincerity.

Covey, Steven: Author of *The Seven Habits of Highly Effective People* and co-author of *First Things First*.

Curtis, Kayla: Student.

David, Fred: Author of *Strategic Management: Concepts and Cases*.

David, Jack: Owner of ECW Press.

Diamond, Stuart: Author of *Getting More*.

Diller, Barry: Chairman and senior executive of IAC/InterActiveCorp and responsible for the creation of Fox Broadcasting.

Dinkin, Greg: Author of *The Poker MBA or the Maverick's Guide to Poker*.

Disney, Walt: A film producer, director, screenwriter, voice actor, animator, and entrepreneur.

Drucker, Peter: One of the best-known management writers in the world.

Duffy, Sean: Congressman.

Duke, Annie: Bracelet winner with over $2 million in winnings. www.dustyschmidt.net.

Dwan, Tom: Known for his aggressive poker play; plays in some of the highest cash games.

Dyer, Jeffrey H., Hal B. Gregersen, and Clayton M. Christense: "The Innovator's DNA," *Harvard Business Review*, December 2009. www.econ.ucsb.edu.

Edison, Thomas: With over 1,000 patents, he invented the phonograph, the motion picture camera, and the electric lightbulb.

Eike, Hope: Student.

Einstein, Albert: The father of modern physics.

Eisenhower, Dwight: 34th president of the United States.

Eisner, Michael: CEO of Disney.

Ellison, Larry: CEO of Oracle.

Faust, Gerry: Great practical business speaker and CEO of Faust Management Corporation.

Favre, Brett: The only quarterback in NFL history to throw for over 70,000 yards, over 500 touchdowns, and over 300 interceptions.

Ferguson, Chris: PhD in computer science, with over $4.5 million in tournament winnings.

Fishman, Steve: "The Madoff Tapes," *New York Magazine*, 27 February 2011.

Fortune Magazine, "Airline King," 2 May 2011.

Foss, Kyle: Student.

Franklin, Benjamin: One of the founding fathers of the United States. Author, printer, politician, postmaster, scientist, inventor, and diplomat.

Friedberg, Jon: WSOP bracelet winner and CEO of Reactrix Systems.

Fritz, Madeline: Student.

Fudd, Elmer: Looney Tunes cartoon character. When he speaks, he replaces Rs and Ls with Ws.

Gardner, Christopher: Entrepreneur, motivational speaker, and author of *The Pursuit of Happyness*.

Gates, Bill: Chairman of Microsoft. Entrepreneur of the personal computer revolution. More importantly, he donates large amounts of money to various charitable organizations.

Gekko, Gordon: Main anti-hero of the *Wall Street* films.

Gelatt, Philip: President of Northern Engraving.

Gilkey, Roderick, Ricardo Caceda, and Clinton Kilts: "When Emotional Reasoning Trumps IQ: Interaction," *Harvard Business Review*, September 2001.

Gillman, J. and White, S.: Authors of *Business Plans That Work*.

Giuffre, Nate: Student.

Gold, Jamie: Television producer, talent agent, and poker player. Winner of the WSOP main event.

www.goodreads.com/author/quotes/61105Dr_Seuss.

Gordon, Phil: Netsys executive, finisher at several WSOP final tables, commentator, and poker author.

Gow, Joe: Chancellor of the University of Wisconsin-La Crosse.

Grace, W.R.: William Russell was founder of W.R. Grace and Company and mayor of New York.

Gratzner, David: Manhattan Institute scholar.

Green, Julien: Author of *Each in His Own Darkness*.

Greenstein, Barry: Acquisition negotiator for Symantec and winner of over $7 million in poker tournaments.

Gretzky, Wayne: Generally regarded as the best hockey player.

Hamel, Gary and C.K. Prahalad: "Competing for the Future," *Harvard Business Review*, January–February 1989.

Hamel, Gary, Yves L. Doz, and C.K. Prahalad: "Collaborate with Your Competitors — and Win," *Harvard Business Review*, January–February 1989.

Hanson, Eric: Student.

Harding, Warren G.: 29th president of the United States.

Hardy, Roger: CEO of Coastal Contacts.

www.harley-davidson.com.

Harrington, Dan: Professional poker player and author.

Harrison, Rick: On television program *Pawn Stars*.

www.h-dsn.com/genbus.

Hellmuth, Phil: Holds a record 11 WSOP bracelets.

Hench, Tom: Department chair, University of Wisconsin–La Crosse.

Henisz, Witold J. and A. Zelner Bennet: "The Hidden Risks in Emerging Markets," *Harvard Business Review*, April 2010.

Henningfield, Drew: Student.

Hensburg, Theodore: President emeritus of Notre Dame.

Hill, Napoleon: Author of *Think and Grow Rich*, one of the best-selling books of all time.

Holmes, Sherlock: A fictional brilliant London detective created by Scottish author and physician Sir Arthur Conan Doyle.

Holtz, Lou: Football coach, sportscaster, author, and motivational speaker.

www.homedepot.com.

Hood, John B.: Confederate general during the American Civil War.

Horne, Scott: Judge in La Cross County, Wisconsin.

Horovitz, Bruce: Interview in *USA*, 7 March 2011.

Horwath, Rich: Strategic thinking speaker and author of *Strategy for You*.

Hsieh, Tony: CEO of Zappos.com.

Hubner, Casey: Student.

Huinker, Ryan: Bank executive and talented writer. He also came up with the title of this book, *The Shark and the Fish*.

www.ibm.com/smarterplanet.

Ivey, Phil: Winner of eight WSOP bracelets. Regarded as the best all-around player in the world.

Jackson, Phil: Professional basketball player and considered one of the greatest coaches ever, with 11 NBA titles.

Jansen, Corey: Student.

Jobs, Steve: Former Apple CEO.

Johnson, Lyndon B.: 36th president of the United States.

Johnson, Major Robert: World War II fighter pilot.

Keynes, John Maynard: Economist and proponent of the concept that government should intervene to fix economic problems.

Kissinger, Henry: National security adviser and secretary of state. Won the Nobel Peace Prize.

Kiyosaki, Robert: Author of *Rich Dad*.

Klein, Denny: CEO of Hydrogen Technology Applications. Invented aqugen.

Knight, Charles: Former chairman of Emerson Electric.

Krohn, A.: Author of *Hooked on Learning: The Roots of Motivation in the Classroom*.

Krzyzewski, Mike: Men's college basketball coach of the Duke Blue Devils.

Kueffel, Tom: Former department chair, University of Wisconsin–La Crosse.

Laliberte, Guy: Founder of Cirque du Soleil. Finished fourth in a WPT championship and won almost $700,000.

Lay, Ken: Known for his role in the corruption scandal that led to the downfall of Enron.

Leahy, Jack: Student.

Lederer, Howard: Over $5.9 million in tournament winnings and two-time WSOP bracelet winner.

Lee, Peggy: Singer, songwriter, actress.

Lehr, Lewis: CEO of 3M.

LeJune, Steve: Author of *Profiles of the World's Best CEOs*, www.barrons.com.

Levine, Elliott: Judge in La Crosse County, Wisconsin.

Lewin, Kurt: Boone and Kurtz, *Contemporary Marketing*.

Lim, Louisa: "Hot Pot, Delivered: In China, a New Dining Experience," National Public Radio, 22 April 2011.

Lincoln, Abraham: 16th president of the United States.

Link, Terry: Associated Press.

Linn, A.: "Crowded Coupon Industry Competes for Users," www.today.msnbc.msn.com, 10 March 2011.

Lombardi, Vince: Green Bay Packers football coach. The NFL Super Bowl trophy is named in his honor.

Luke: Paul Newman's character in *Cool Hand Luke*.

Lussier, Achua: Author of *Leadership*.

Ma, Yo-Yo: Cellist and composer. Winner of several Grammy Awards.

MacMillan, Douglas: "Careers," *Bloomberg Businessweek*, 18 June 2008.

Madoff, Andrew: Bernard Madoff's son.

Madoff, Bernard: Operator of the largest Ponzi scheme (outside of Social Security) in history.

May, Bruce: Dean of the College of Business, University of Wisconsin–La Crosse.

www.mayoclinic.com

McAllister, Bill: Retired CEO of Colonial Mechanical Corporation and old friend.

McCauley, Pat: Susquehanna International Group.

McConnell, David: To attract female customers when he was selling books door to door, he gave away small bottles of perfume. The company became Avon.

McEvoy, Tom: Winner of the WSOP main event.

McManus, James: Author of *Cowboys Full*, *Positively Fifth Street*, and *Binion's World Series of Poker*.

Melby, Nathan: Student.

www.microsoft.com/about/en/us/default.aspx.

Milken, Michael: Developer of many junk bonds. Pleaded guilty to violating U.S. security laws.

Mill, John Stuart: British philosopher. Favored individual freedom and opposed state control.

Mohajeri, Kia: Consistent placer in many tournaments, with over $1 million in poker winnings.

www.money.cnn.com.

Morrison, Kirk: WSOP champion.

Mother Teresa: Catholic nun. Founded the Missionaries of Charity in Calcutta. She won the Nobel Peace Prize for her humanitarian work.

www.myersbriggs.org.

Napster: Shawn Fanning created a file-sharing music platform.

Navarro, Joe: Former FBI agent and author of *What Every Body Is Saying*.

Negreanu, Daniel: Canadian professional poker player. Winner of four WSOP bracelets. At one time ranked first in all-time career earnings.

Nesson, Charlie: Harvard law professor and founder of the Global Poker Strategic Thinking Society.

Newton, Barry: Managing director of global sales and marketing for UST Global.

Nicklaus, Jack: Professional golfer. Won 18 major championships. Regarded as one of the greatest professional golfers of all time.

Nieto, Augie: Founder and retired CEO of Life Fitness.

Nighbor, Matt: Student.

Nightingale, Earl: Motivational speaker. Author of *The Strangest Secret*.

Nixon, Richard: 37th president of the United States.

Noyce, Jerry: Good friend and CEO of Health Fitness Corporation and other companies. Also known for his great tennis coaching. Member of the Tennis Hall of Fame.

Ones, Deinz, and Stephan Dilchert: "How Special Are Executives?," *Industrial and Organizational Psychology*, 2009.

O'Toole, J., and W. Bennis: "What's Needed Next: A Culture of Candor," *Harvard Business Review*, June 2009.

Ovitz, Michael: Talent agent. Co-founded Creative Artists Agency and served as its chairman; also served as president of the Walt Disney Company.

Pareto, Vilfredo: Italian engineer, sociologist, economist, and philosopher who came up with the 80/20 rule.

Patrick, Craig: Fox News.

Patton, George: Brilliant controversial Army general in World War II.

Pearl, Bill: Good friend. Bill won the Mr. Universe contest several times and became a trainer and author on the subject.

Pickens, T. Boone: American financier who chairs the hedge fund BP Capital Management.

Pisapia, John: Author of *The Strategic Leader*.

www.poker.com/poker-pros/tom-mcevoy-poker-pro.htm.

www.pokervt.com.

PostOakBluff Internet video.

Pozen, Robert C.: "The Case for Professional Boards," *Harvard Business Review*, December 2010.

Powell, Colin: Chairman of the Joint Chiefs of Staff and 65th secretary of state.

Prasad, R.: "The Hindu," 12 August 2010, clear-concepts.in/blog.

Quelch, John A., and Katherine E. Jocz: "How to Market in a Downturn," *Harvard Business Review*, April 2009.

Quillin, Phil: CEO of Quillin's Groceries.

Rand, Barry: CEO of Avis and AARP.

Raymer, Greg: Pfizer attorney and WSOP main event champion.

Reagan, Ronald: 40th president of the United States.

Reardon, M. Marguerite: "Cisco, Microsoft: Cozy Competitors," CNET News, 20 August 2007.

Redleaf, Andy: CEO of the $4 billion hedge fund Whitebox Advisors.

Reese, Chip: Professional poker player; regarded as the best cash game player in the world.

Reineke, Dan: Student.

www.retailindustry.com/about.

Robbins, Tony: Success coach and author of *Unlimited Power: The New Science of Personal Achievement* and *Awaken the Giant Within*.

Roberto, Michael: Author of *Art of Critical Decision Making*, audiobook, the Great Courses.

Robinson, Danon: Toro trading partner.

Roosevelt, Franklin D.: 32nd president of the United States.

Rosenblatt, Daniel: Student.

Rowekamp, Tyler: Student.

Rubens, Ron: Creator of the World Poker Tour Camp.

Russell, Bill: Professional basketball player who played center for the Boston Celtics.

Russell, Keri: Actress and dancer. Golden Globe award winner.

www.samples-help.org.uk.

www.sbinformation.about.com.

Scarface: Fictional Cuban immigrant, played by Al Pacino, who takes over a drug empire in the movie of the same name.

Schmidt, Dusty: Winner of over $4 million online.

Schukar, Doug: CEO of USA Mortgage.

Schultz, Howard: CEO of Starbucks.

Schulze, Richard: Founder of Best Buy.

Schussler, Stephen: Founder of Rainforest Café.

Seidel, Eric: Winner of eight WSOP bracelets and over $16 million in tournament winnings.

Seif, Mark: Professional poker player.

Sexton, Mike: True gentleman, host of the World Poker Tour, member of the Poker Hall of Fame, WSOP bracelet winner, with over $3.8 million in tournament winnings. Most importantly, Mike donates half of his tournament winnings to charity and was a co-founder of Poker Gives, a charity for poker players to donate some of their winnings.

Shelton, Hugh: Warrior, former chairman of the Joint Chiefs of Staff.

Sherman, William T.: General in the Union Army during the Civil War. Known for his military strategy and his "scorched earth" march against the South.

Sinek, Simon: Author and marketing consultant.

Sklansky, David: Professional poker player and author.

Smisek, Jeff: CEO of United Airlines and United Continental Holdings.

Smith, Adam: Economist and proponent of the concept that people working in their own self-interest will result in good market outcomes.

Smith, Fred: CEO of Federal Express.

Socrates: Renowned for his contribution to philosophy and ethics.

Spock: The logical Vulcan, second in command in the original *Star Trek* series.

www.starbucks.com.

Stewart, Martha: Television personality and entrepreneur.

Straus, Jack: During the Poker World Championship, he was down to one chip and won the tournament. Known for the saying "a chip and a chair."

Sullenberger, Sully: Landed his plane on the Hudson River, saving every passenger.

Sun Tzu: Chinese military general. Believed to have authored *The Art of War*.

Swayne, Brian: One of my sons. He pilots Tomcats and Super Hornets and has been a Wall Street equities trader.

Swayne, Carol: Wonderful wife.

Swayne, Chuck: One of my sons. He played on the professional tennis tour and is now a property investor and manager in the Cincinnati area.

Swayne, Joe: One of my sons. He ran the family business for years, is a many-degreed black belt, and has owned his own karate studio.

Tarkenton, Fran: Quarterback for the Vikings and TV personality.

www.tgci.com/magazine.shtml.

www.theglobeandmail.com.

www.thinkexist.com.

Tracy, Brian: CEO of Brian Tracy International. Self-help author and speaker on leadership, sales, managerial effectiveness, and business strategy. Brian is a personal favorite and a true gentleman.

Truman, Harry: 33rd president of the United States.

Trump, Donald: Chairman and CEO of the Trump Organization, a real-estate developer. Also operates numerous casinos and hotels.

Turner, Ted: Founder of CNN. Media mogul and, most importantly, philanthropist.

Twain, Mark: Author and humorist. Most noted for his novels *The Adventures of Tom Sawyer* and *The Adventures of Huckleberry Finn*.

Uhler, Frank: Great lifetime friend, so-so racquetball player, former general partner of Alexander Grant, and CEO of La Crosse Footwear.

www.valuebasedmanagement.net.

Vroman, Tony: Student.

Walters, Billy: *60 Minutes*.

Wasicka, Paul: Runner-up at the WSOP main event and winner of the NBC National Heads-Up Poker Championship.

Welch, Jack: Chairman of General Electric.

Watson: IBM's artificial intelligence computer.

Widuch, Dan: Lecturer, life adventurer, and founder of Be Alive Network.

Wilde, Oscar: Irish author and playwright.

Winfrey, Oprah: Actress, owner of her own television network, and talk-show host. Most importantly, known as the greatest black philanthropist in American history.

Wooden, John: Basketball player and coach.

Wright, James: Inventor of Silly Putty.

Youg, Nam: Former CEO of LG Electronics.

www.youngentrepreneur.com.

Zamperini, Louis: World War II prisoner of war survivor, inspirational speaker, and former American Olympic distance runner.